AF573858

VISIONS OF ILLINOIS

VISIONS OF ILLINOIS

A series of publications portraying the rich heritage of the state through historical and contemporary works of photography and art

BOOKS IN THE SERIES

Prairiescapes *Photographs by Larry Kanfer*

Nelson Algren's Chicago *Photographs by Art Shay*

Stopping By: Portraits from Small Towns *Photographs by Raymond Bial*

Changing Chicago: A Photodocumentary

Chicago and Downstate: Illinois as Seen by the Farm Security Administration Photographers, 1936-1943 *Edited by Robert L. Reid and Larry A. Viskochil*

The Many Faces of Hull-House: The Photographs of Wallace Kirkland *Edited by Mary Ann Johnson*

Beneath an Open Sky *Panoramic Photographs by Gary Irving*

Billy Morrow Jackson: Interpretations of Time and Light *Howard E. Wooden*

Beneath an Open Sky

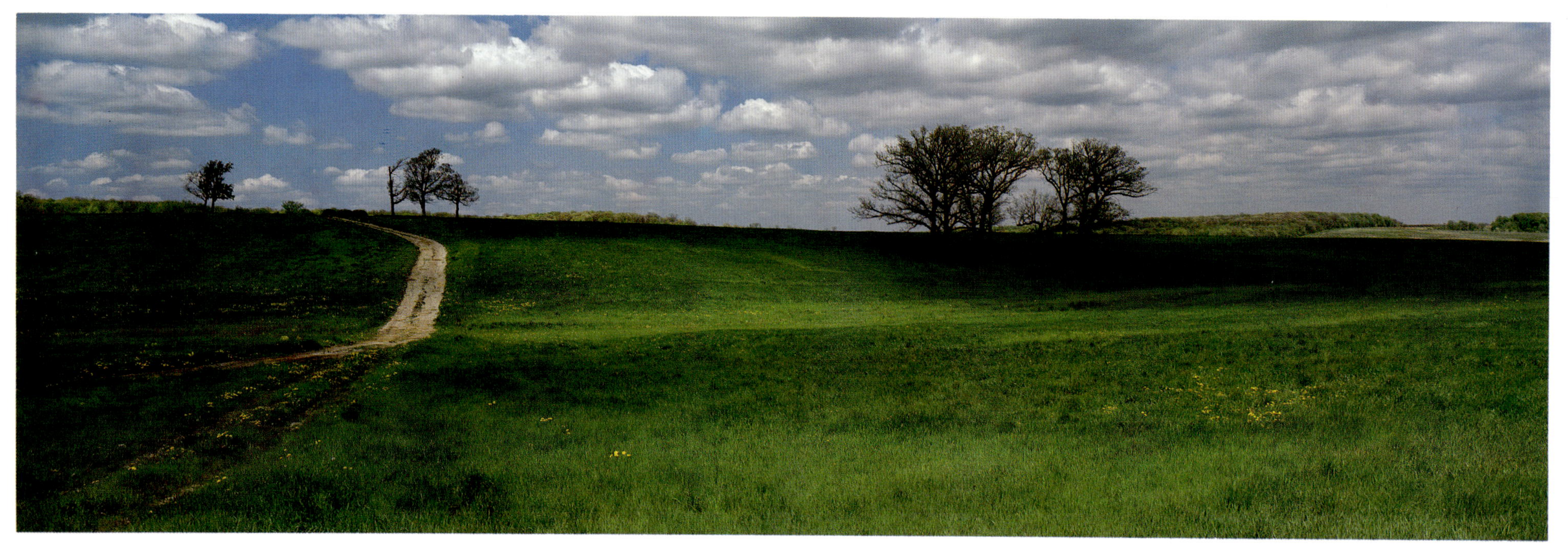

Beneath an Open Sky

Panoramic Photographs by Gary Irving

With an Introduction by Raymond Bial

University of Illinois Press *Urbana and Chicago*

Manufactured in Japan
C 5 4 3 2 1

Library of Congress Cataloging-in-Publication Data

Irving, Gary.
Beneath an open sky : panoramic photographs / by Gary Irving.
p. cm. — (Visions of Illinois)
ISBN 0-252-01649-1 (alk. paper)
1. Illinois—Description and travel—1981- —Views. 2. Landscape—Illinois—Pictorial works. I. Title. II. Series.
F542.I67 1990
917.73—dc20 90-10760
CIP

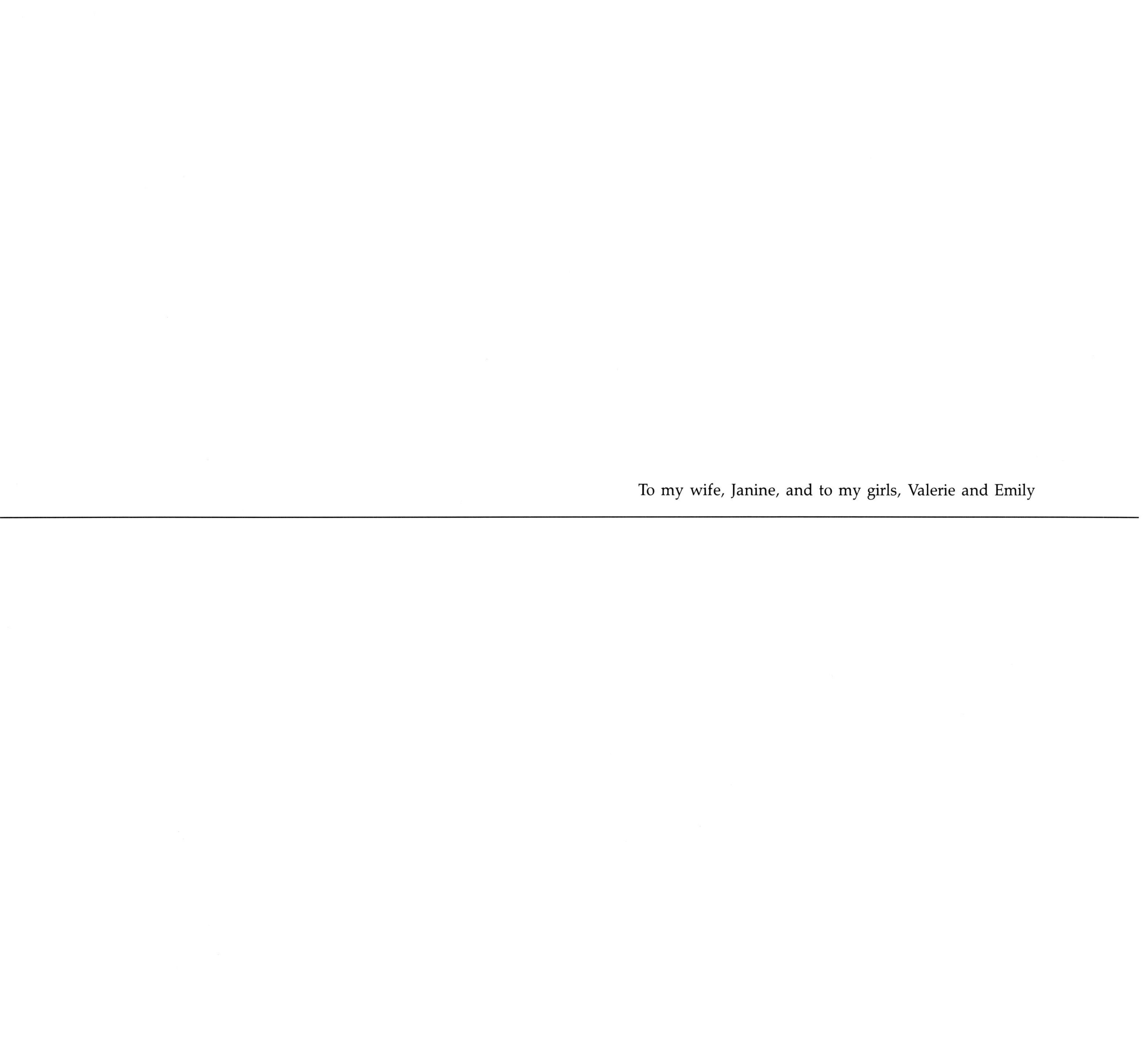

To my wife, Janine, and to my girls, Valerie and Emily

The health of the eye seems to demand a horizon. We are never tired, so long as we can see far enough. EMERSON

PREFACE

I remember the very first time I saw images that really moved me. I was a high-school student with an interest in science fiction and had gone with some friends to one of those now rare theaters with a wide, curved screen. There in the darkened theater I found myself gazing up in wonder at some of the most spectacular landscapes I had ever seen, sweeping panoramic views of the African veldt in the beginning sequence of the film *2001: A Space Odyssey.* Memories of those brief but powerful images were influential in my subsequent pursuit of landscape photography as a vocation.

As a landscape photographer located in the Midwest, I am often asked by colleagues from more scenic regions if I find it frustrating to live in an area so devoid of any apparent visual interest. Up until just a few years ago, I shared their unfortunate disregard of the unheralded beauty of this region. While I have traveled with the camera to almost every part of the country, it wasn't until 1987 when a publisher from Oregon commissioned me to photograph images for a book on Illinois that I really began to discover the pleasures of the open landscape. Here were scenes that in many ways recalled those wide African views from years before.

I find that the excitement of the light-swept landscape off some Illinois back road recalls the very same feeling I experience when I stand on a Pacific Coast overlook or when I hike deep into the mist-enshrouded hardwood forests of New England. The beauty of this place is the kind that grows on you, the kind that holds rewards for those willing to look beyond the obvious and learn the vernacular of Midwestern light.

This collection of photographs is an attempt to convey my affection for the broad landscape of rural Illinois. Using the Panorama camera, I have found it possible to capture the sweep of the horizon as well as to explore the glorious light that radiates across the open land, constantly changing from season to season.

Though the images are intended to celebrate the beauty of the region in its various forms, I do not pretend that they reflect any of the serious issues that confront this part of the world. I believe that beauty is a common grace bestowed upon man, transcending the changes in the human condition. These are personal images that draw upon my own boyhood experiences of summer on my grandparents' farm in Nebraska as well as influences and events that consciously or not have affected my response to the land. My hope is that if they ring true to me, they will strike a familiar chord in you as well.

Perhaps you will take the time to enjoy the simple pleasure of driving along some Midwestern back road, pulling off to the side, and simply looking out over the land, beneath an open sky.

GARY IRVING
Wheaton, Illinois

INTRODUCTION

As a photographer, I have most often seen the Midwest as primarily sky, the land forming a thin line at the bottom edge of most scenes. A noon sun on the plains stands very high, and the blue of a clear day reaches literally to infinity. Storm clouds building on a hot summer afternoon reach towering heights. In many parts of Illinois the land stretches beneath that sky without interruption, except for the occasional farms scattered like so many shipwrecks on the high seas of prairie long since converted to corn and soybeans.

To me, the sky has always been overwhelming because of its great height. So, when I first became acquainted with Gary Irving over the telephone and he began to discuss his panoramic photographs, I considered them to be little more than a curiosity. The elongated images he described might present unusual horizontal views of the landscape, but to my mind any photograph that compressed the sky could hardly present an authentic view of the plains.

Yet I knew that one can gaze across great distances on those plains, and that the dominant element is most certainly the horizon. No matter in what direction one turns, it is always there, a crease between land and sky. Against the horizontal sweep of the plains, telephone poles, fence rows, and anything else that tends toward the vertical appears most often out of character, at times even fragile.

Some weeks later I happened to meet Irving, who showed me a few of his panoramics, and despite my initial reservations I was impressed by the unique format in which the horizontal lines were strongly emphasized. In fact, the horizon drives strongly across nearly every photograph in this fine book.

The book is aptly named *Beneath an Open Sky.* In Irving's photographs we have long stretches of sky, but the vault of sky is eliminated along with the tendency of the eye to sweep upward. Rather our attention is turned back to ground level, permitting us to view scenes and objects in proper perspective.

People seldom appear in Irving's photographs, and in the rare cases when they do, they are assigned roles of minor significance. This is due partly to the character of the photographer, who prefers to work with a measure of privacy, and also to his view that people are of the least consequence on the landscape. Like the mountains and the oceans, the plains appear so vast that people should be placed in scale, as in Chinese paintings, if they are allowed any presence at all. Indeed, their presence might be construed as an intrusion. In a world increasingly dominated and ravaged by humans, I find the lack of people in Irving's photographs to be a relief.

Actually, on the plains it is weather, both in its variety and in its mood, that matters more than land or people. The ground does vary seasonally from green to black, with an occasional snowfall to brighten the eye. Yet the varieties of cloud formations, the wide range and interplay of colors, subtly presented, and the changing character of the light all combine in a moment to create the magical qualities of a good photograph of the Illinois landscape. A skilled photographer, Gary Irving knows that the finest light and colors appear elusively at dawn when much of the world is asleep, and at dusk when most people are staring at the television. It is no accident that many of the photographs in *Beneath an Open Sky* were made in the delicate light of early morning or evening, with one or two taken in the brooding light of a storm moving across the plain.

Whatever the weather, Illinois is a place in which to be outside is to be truly *outside.* The photographs in this book were clearly made out in the open, where there is no place to conceal oneself. Through them, Irving demonstrates that he has felt the exhilaration of the plains as well as their challenge. He meets every subject head on, or moving with a sweeping gesture from one side to the other. The breadth of the land in these images reminds me very much of what it's like to drive these highways, with not an obstacle in sight, where there is a sense that nearly all things are possible.

This land also has its delicate moments, near ground level, where Queen Anne's lace nods in the wind, leaves of young corn fluctuate with every change in the light, and clouds drag their shadows across the fields. The extreme format of the panoramic photograph, in which the foreground is often shortened and the sky collapsed, emphasizes these details. Many of the photographs in this book assume the intimate, delicate character and calm of still lifes. While all of Irving's photographs employ the wide-angle view of the panoramics, in which the eye is swept expansively from one edge of the frame to the other, there are many photographs in *Beneath an Open Sky* that direct our attention inward to the single light reflecting off the window of a farmhouse, or to the pumpkins pulsing orange in a field bordered by corn.

There is a long tradition of fine landscape photography in America, and a number of photographers have experimented with the panoramic format. Gary Irving is one of the first to work seriously in color with this format over an extended period of time. He has been putting his Fuji camera to good use for several years now, and for this book he spent an entire year in the field, during which he made over eight hundred photographs.

Irving brought all of his skills as a commercial photographer to bear on this project, applying his ability and experience to what is largely an artistic venture. From a purely technical standpoint, all of the photographs in this book are solid, many of them are stunning, and a good number have an enduring quality. What separates Irving's work from the thousands of first-rate commercial photographs cranked out every year by hundreds of other professional photographers? To my mind, knowledge of equipment and processes matter little if not combined with sensitivity and insight—which for lack of a better term I will call the artist's point of view.

I have recently begun to teach my daughter, Anna, about photography, and the first lesson is that photography has nothing to do with film and cameras, which are simply a means to an end. Rather, it amounts to a question of light and imagination and the feeling one has toward one's subjects. We go out at dusk, often hurrying down back roads, and most often when the light is correct we can stop anywhere in the country to experience the mood of the sunset. We are given only a few minutes before a veil of darkness slips over the entire landscape and it is time to head home again. The light has the same special character at dawn. These are brief moments, of a most elusive character, and one is challenged to capture that light. It is most often not found in a specific place, but during a particular moment in which the atmosphere is briefly charged.

Gary Irving knows and respects those moments, choosing to photograph almost exclusively in those brief times in which the light has the proper quality. He has not only taken time to perfect his craft, but in every aspect of his work he demonstrates a deep feeling for his subject. Rising at four A.M. to drive the highways and back roads, anticipating the varying mood of the light, he has worked simply to be there when all the elements come together for a complete photograph. He knows how to accept what he is given, but he also relies upon his own imagination, because good photography often depends not only on what is really there, but also on what we wish to be there. I know a number of artists who work best at dawn and at dusk because in those moments between sleep and waking, one's imagination is most alive.

Looking at this collection of photographs, one can easily imagine oneself standing at the road shoulder, absolutely alone. There is a feeling in many of the photographs that no one else, other than the photographer, is present.

Such is the reward of photographing in the quiet of dawn. To make the photographs, Irving had to leave home in the absolute dark of early morning to drive a hundred or more miles—for what? To ache with cold? To miss his family? To worry about the old car breaking down on an empty stretch of road? It's hard work being a photographer, and good photographs don't simply appear out of thin air. Yet, as Irving knows, it is always worth the sacrifice to have, briefly, the entire landscape to oneself. It is usually no more than an hour, often just a few minutes, before the light changes and the first pickup roars down the blacktop to shatter that mood.

What has Gary Irving given us in *Beneath an Open Sky*? Certainly a stunning collection of photographs, yet on a deeper level he has shared with us many private moments in his life. These photographs tell us a great deal about the Illinois landscape, both literally and metaphorically. However, they reveal to us as much or more about Gary Irving and what he feels about the landscape, including what he gave of himself to make the photographs. One can ask nothing more and nothing less of a fine photographic artist.

RAYMOND BIAL
Urbana, Illinois

Beneath an Open Sky

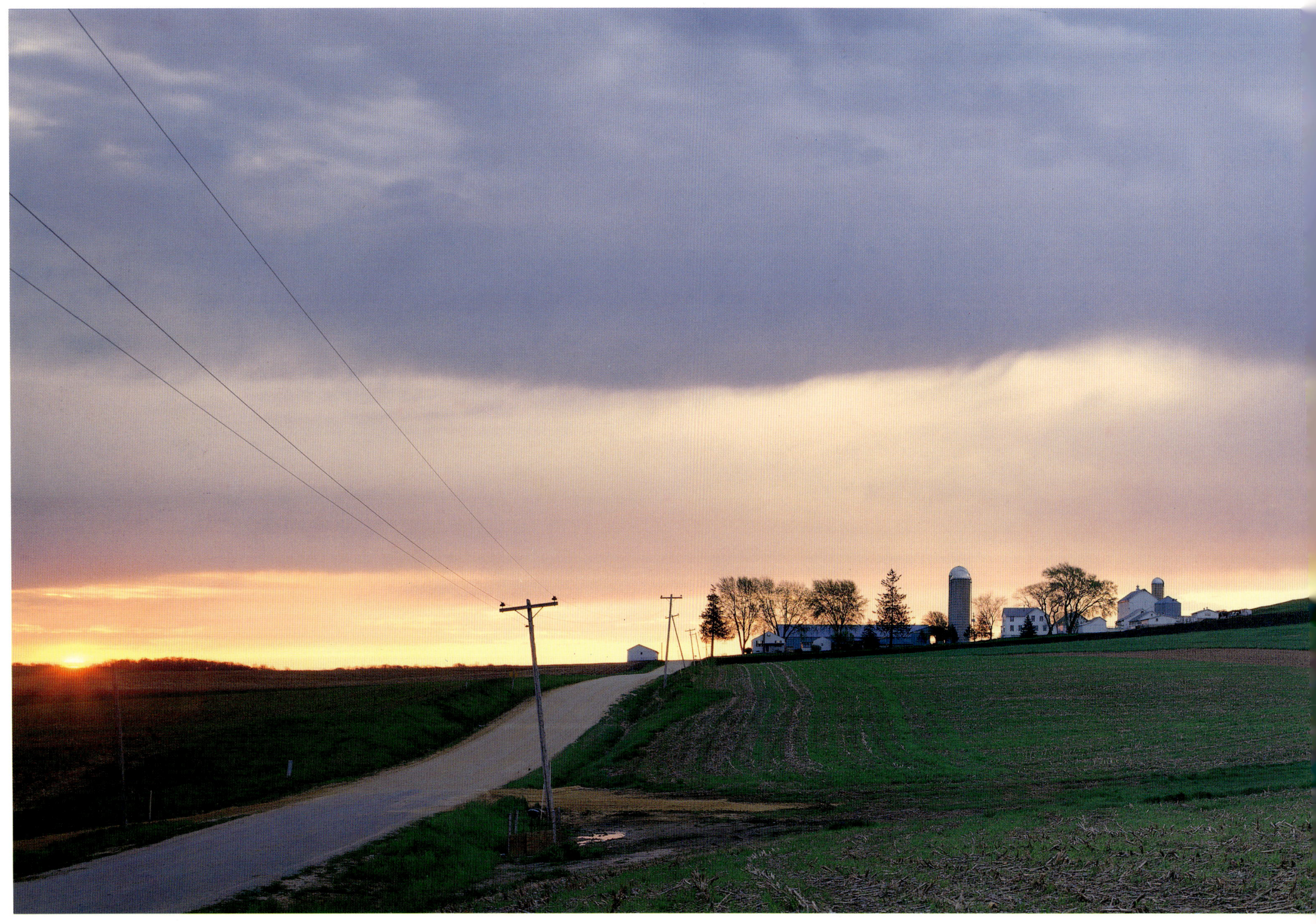

1

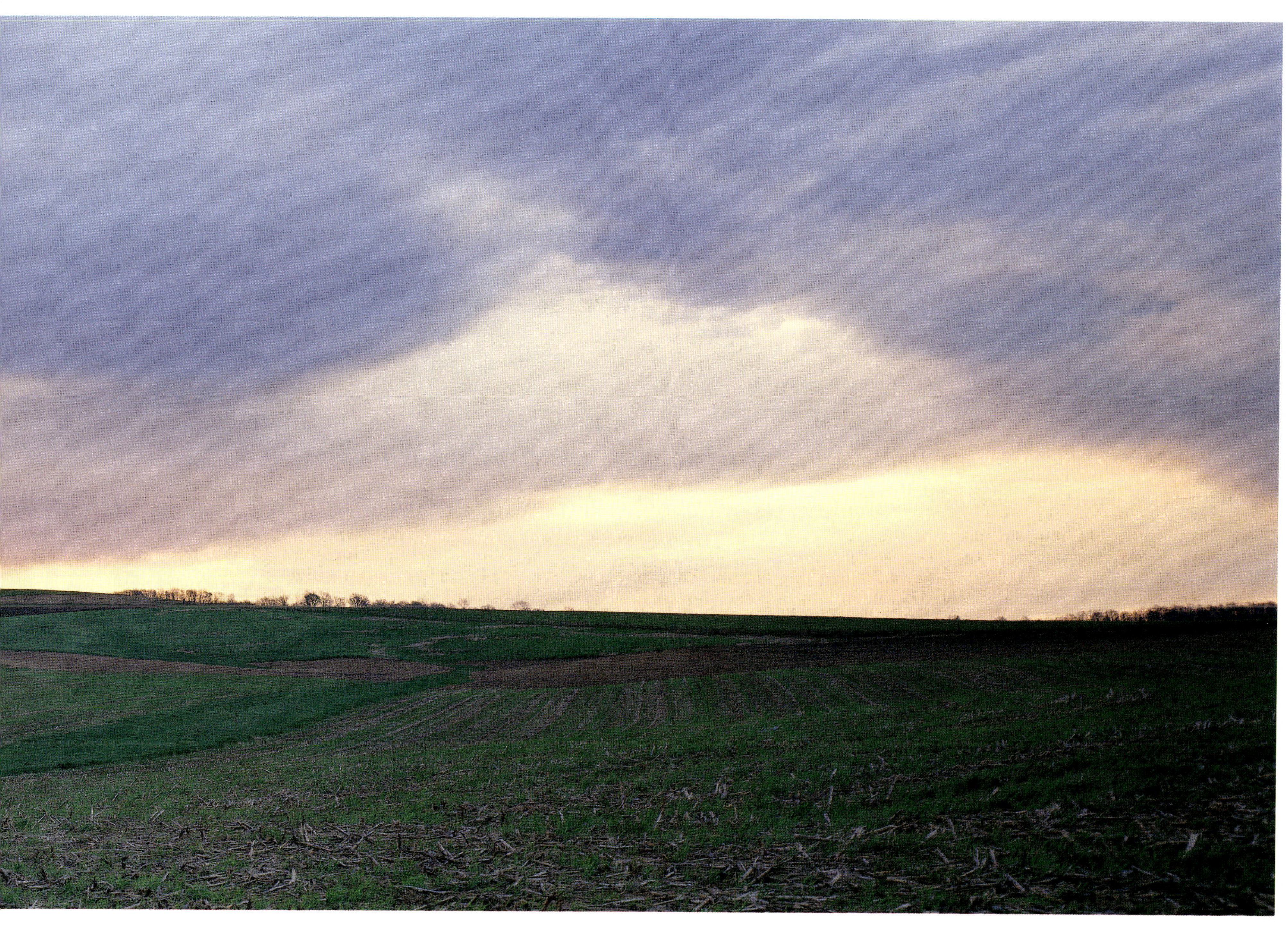

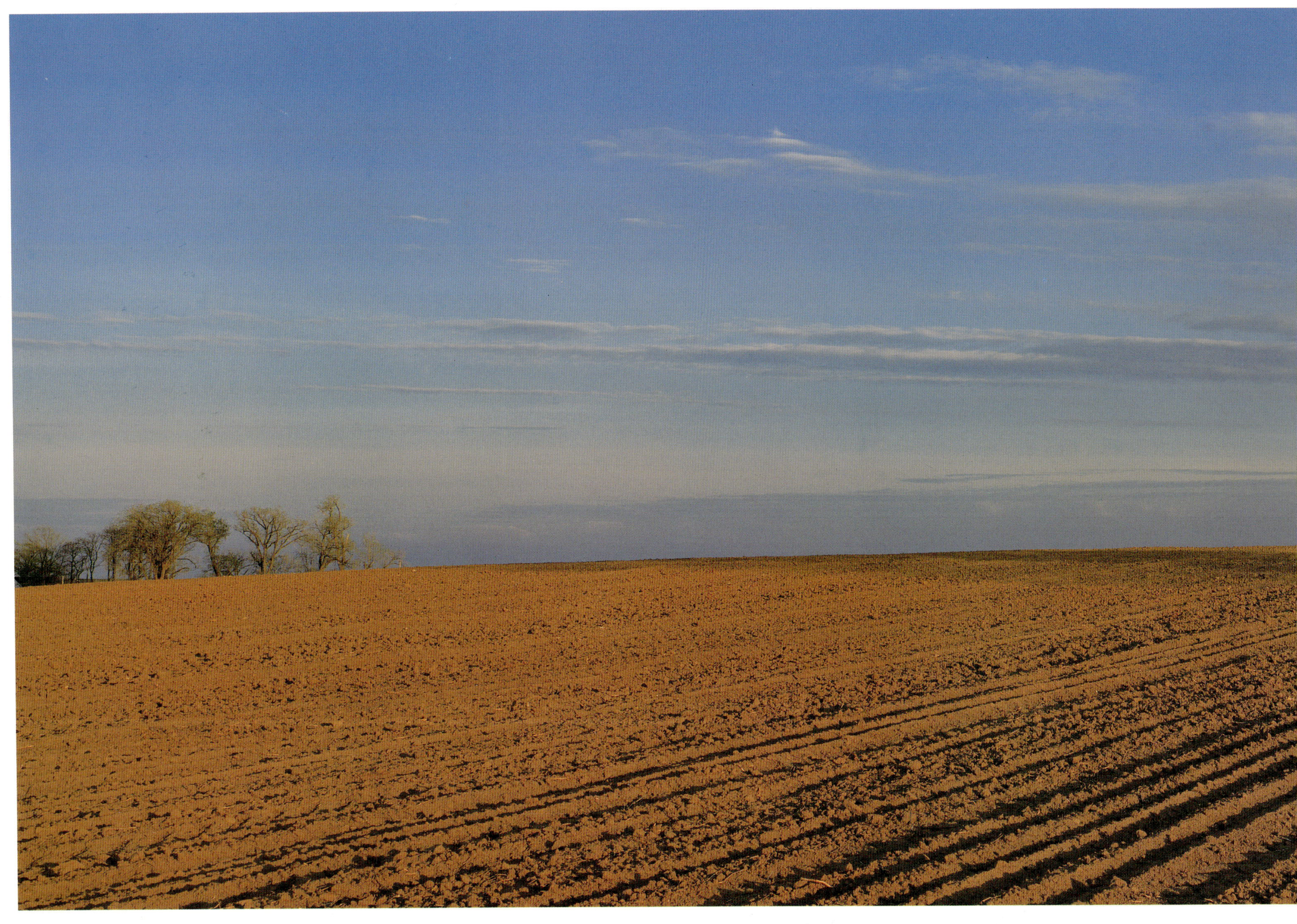

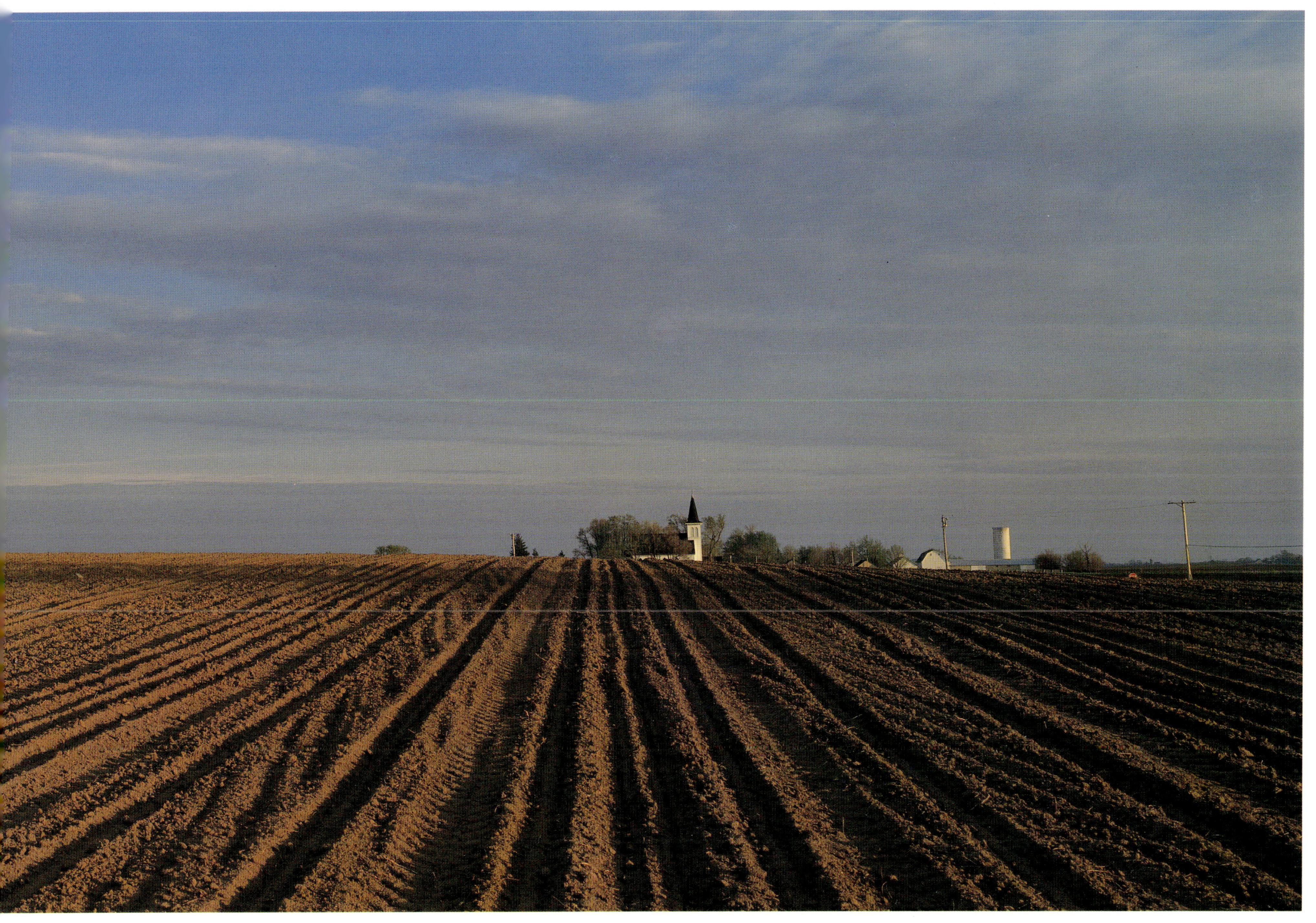

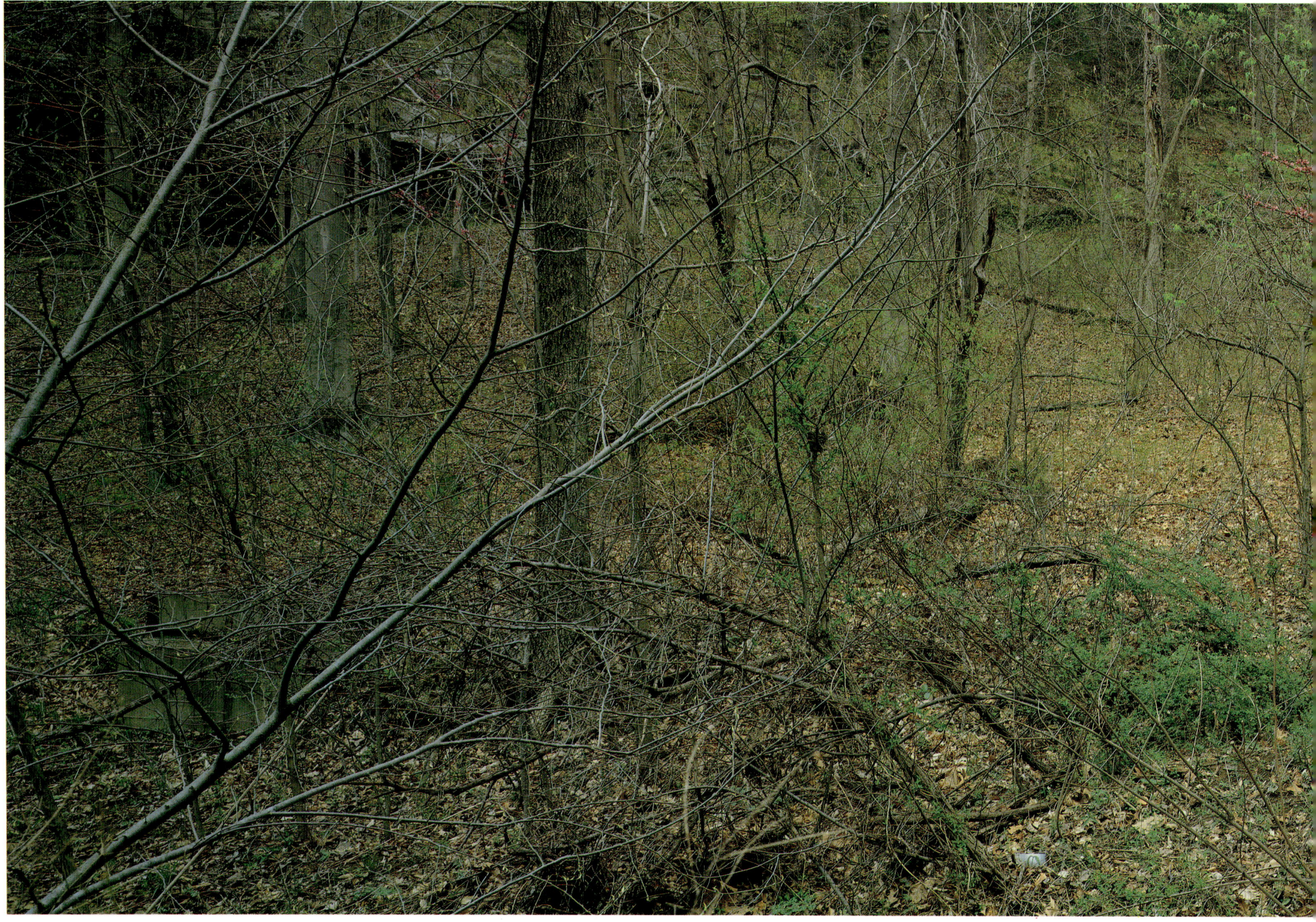

3

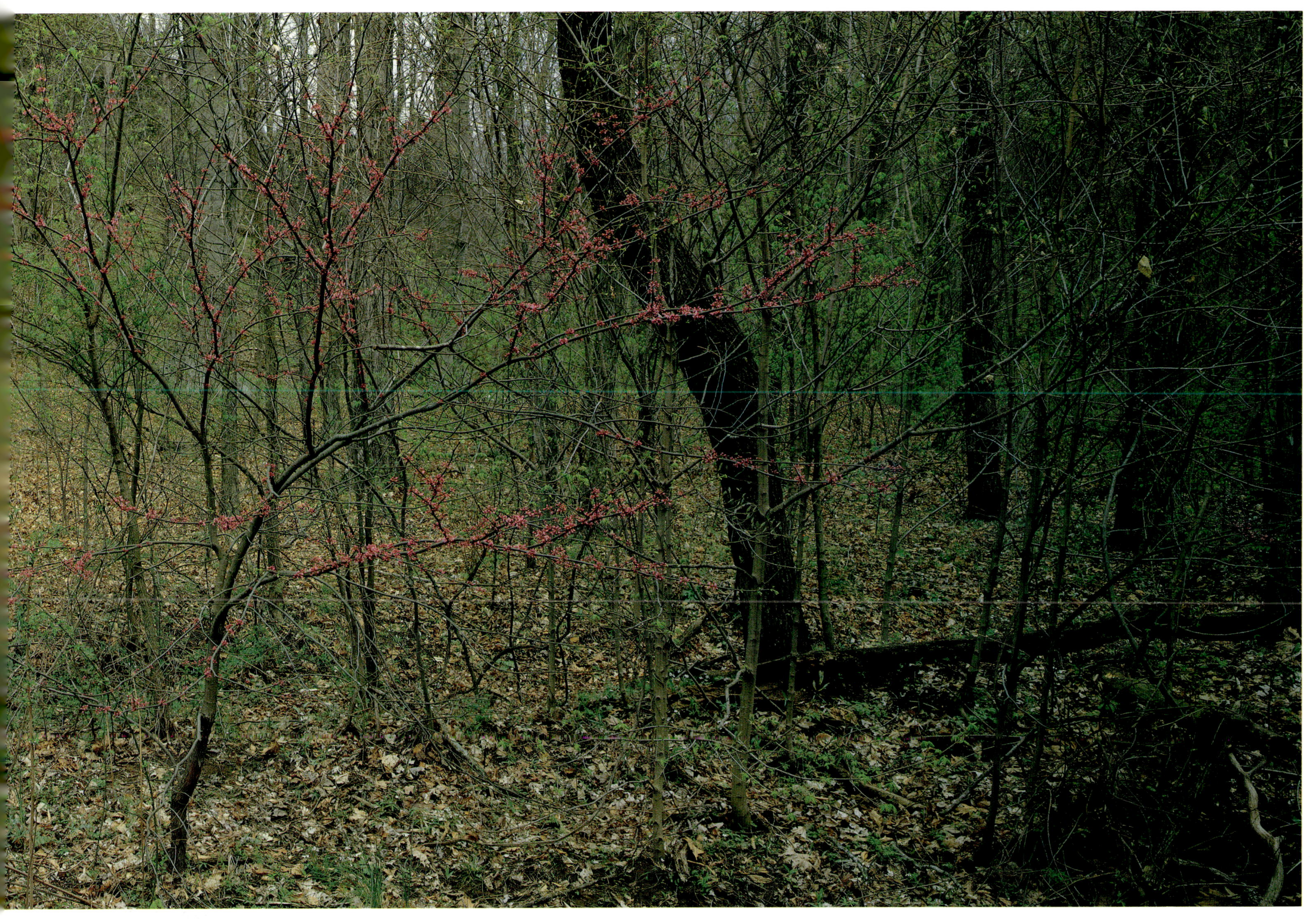

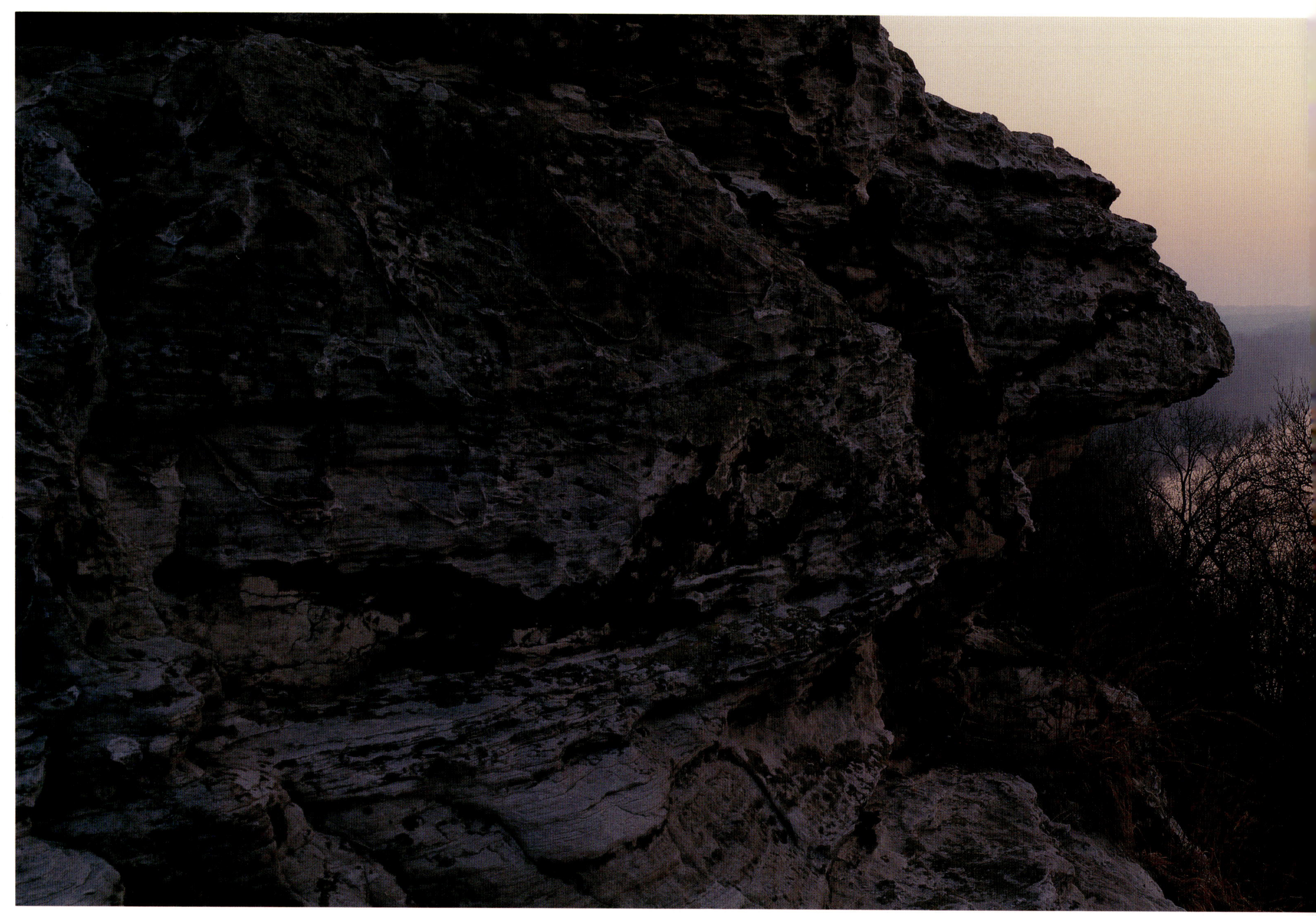

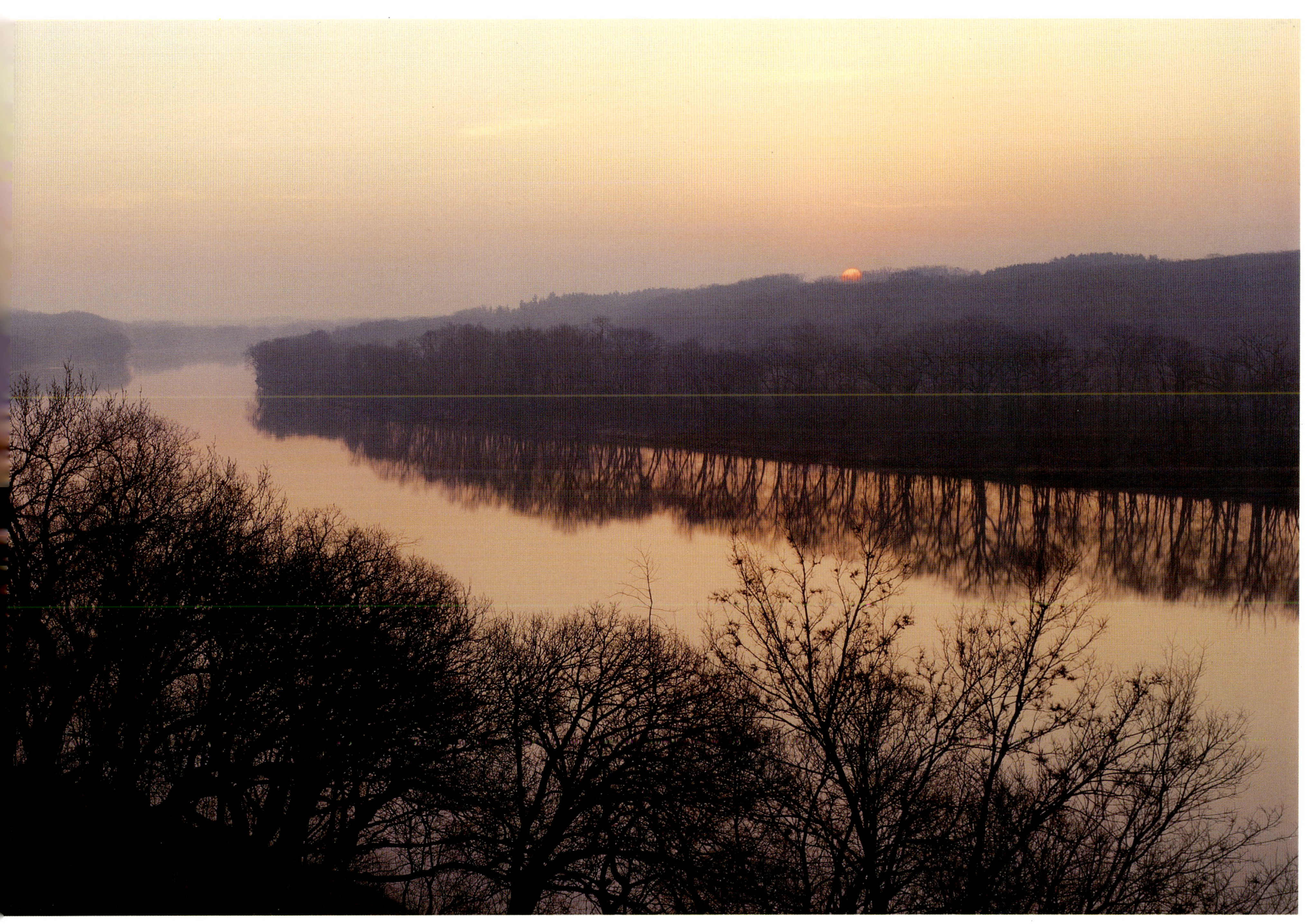

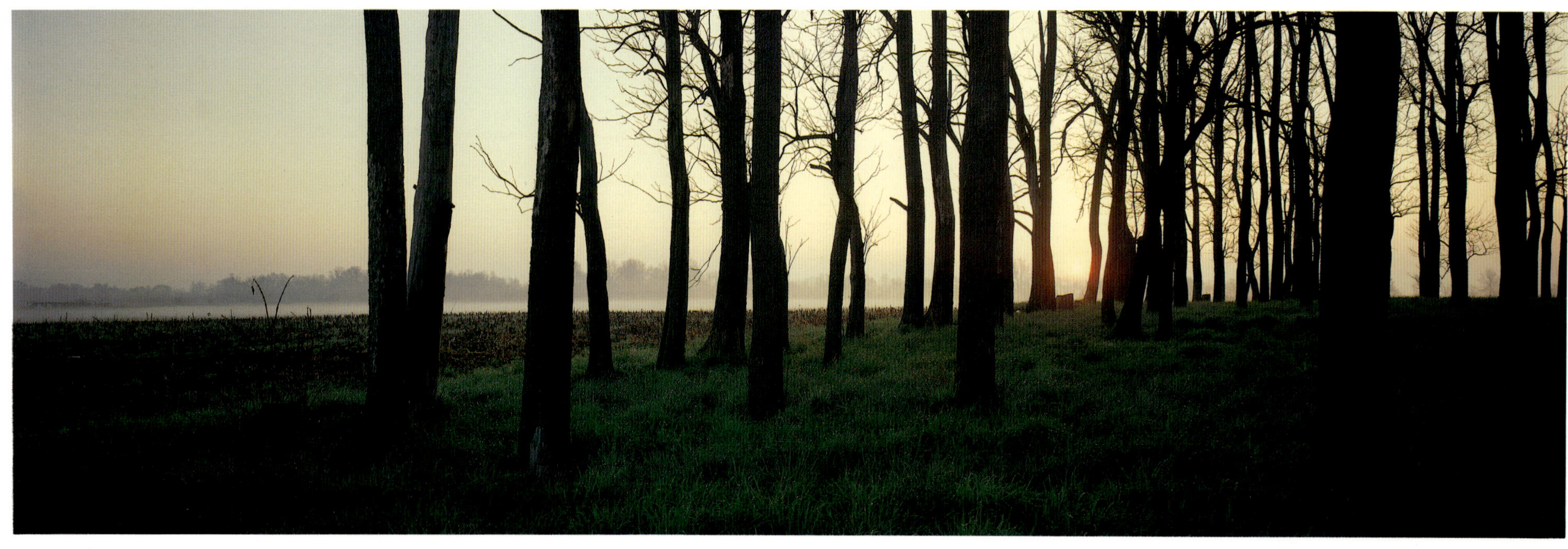

5

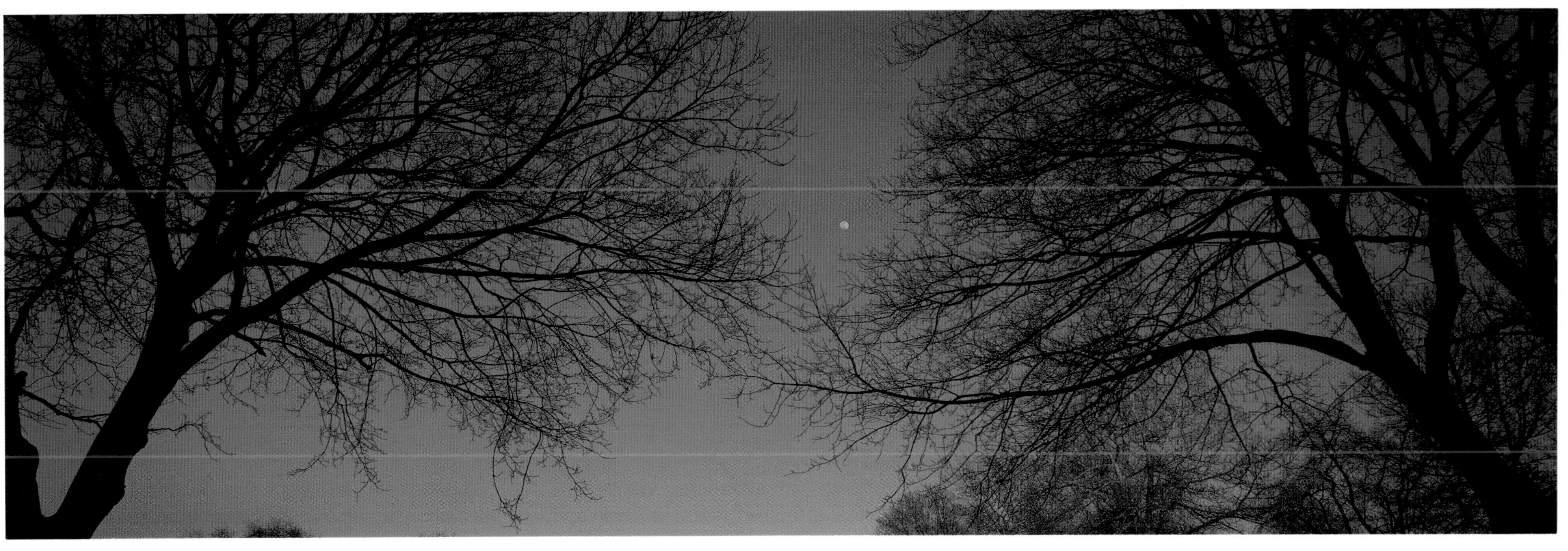

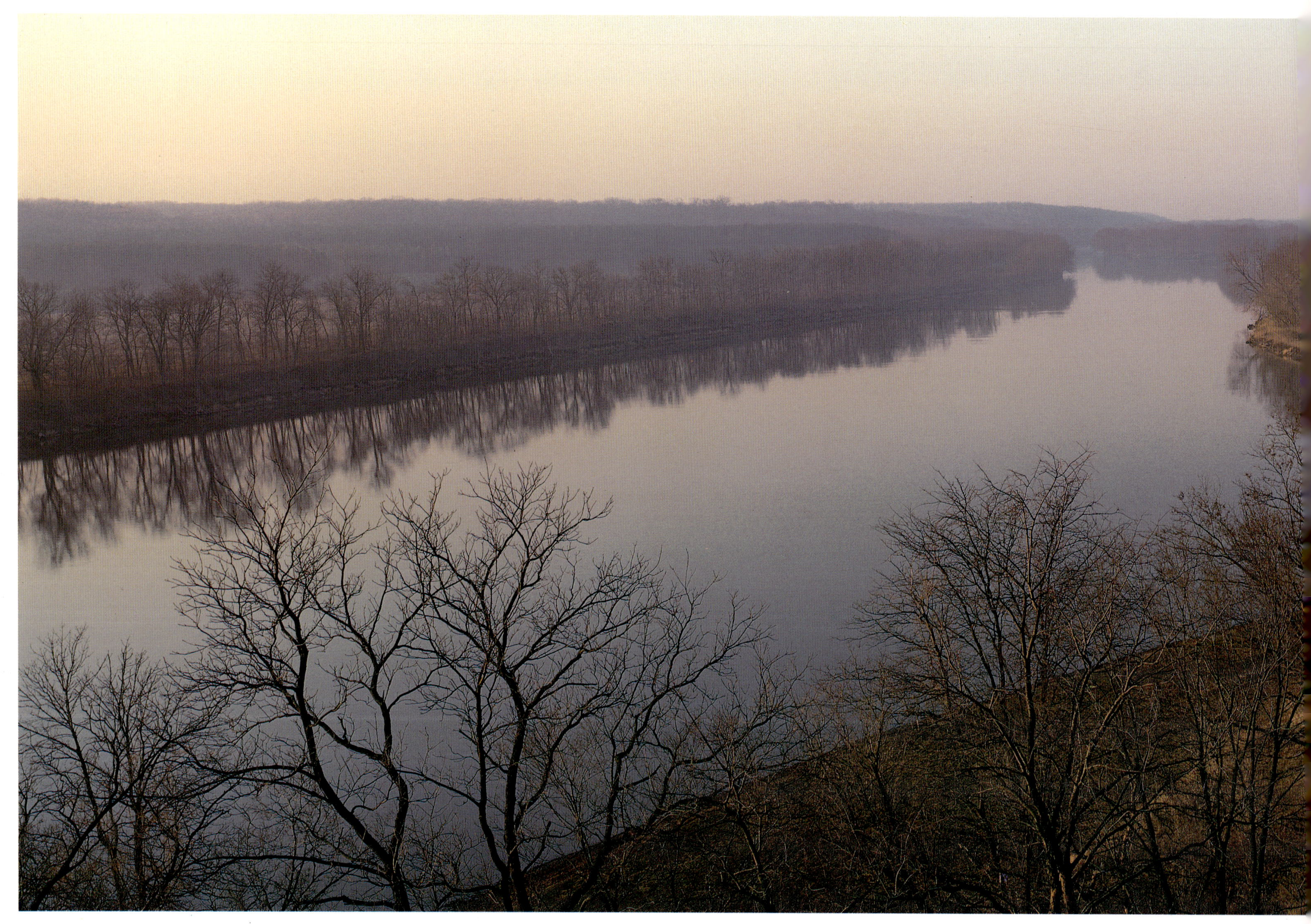

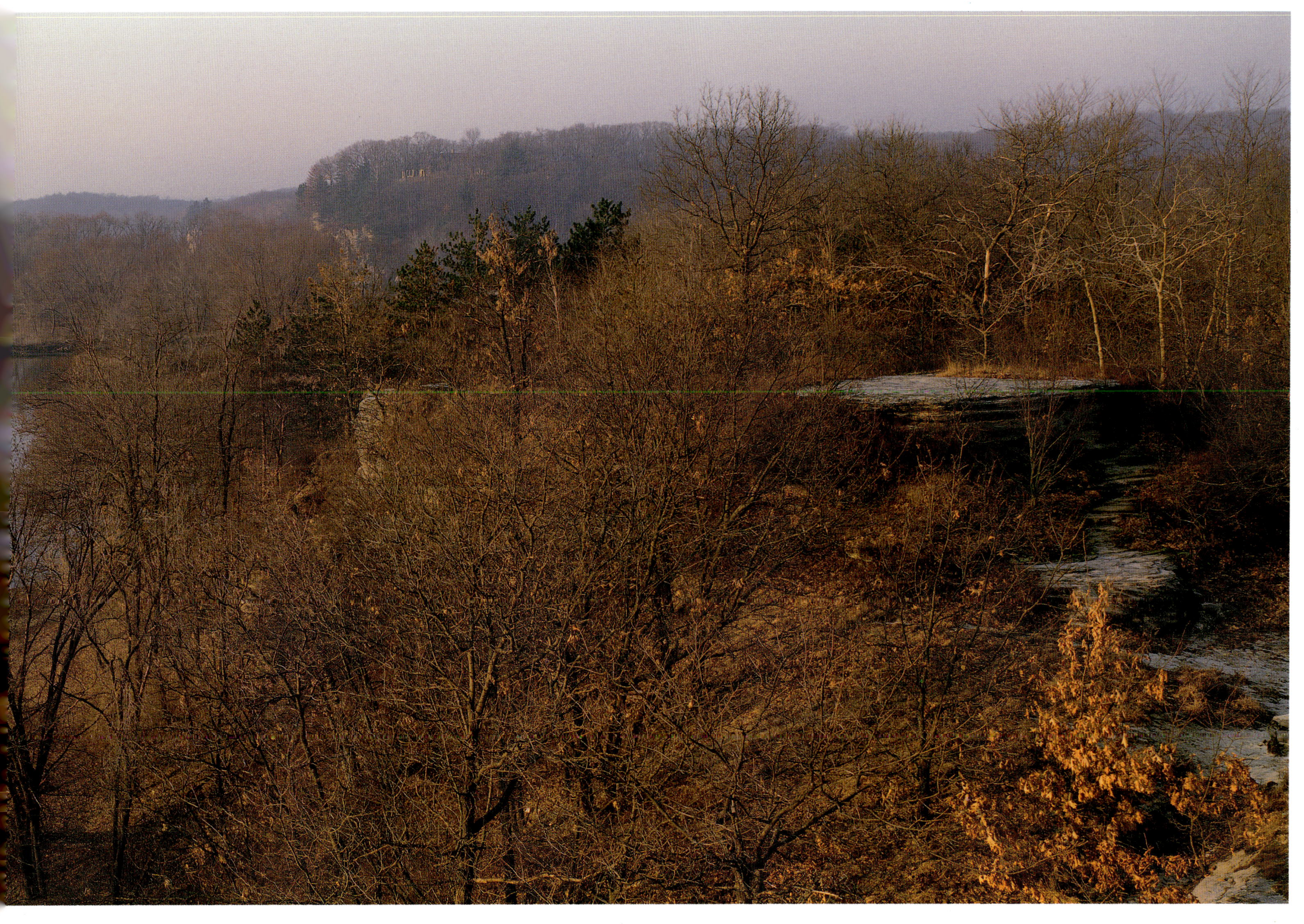

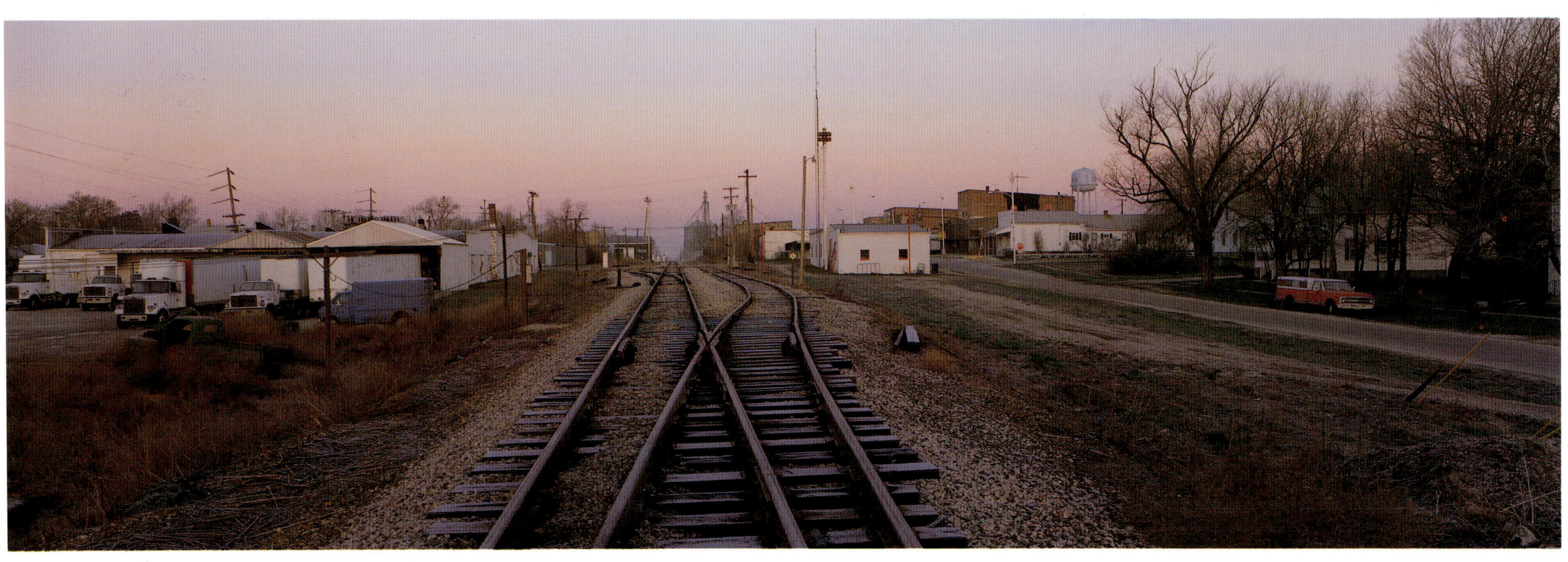

9

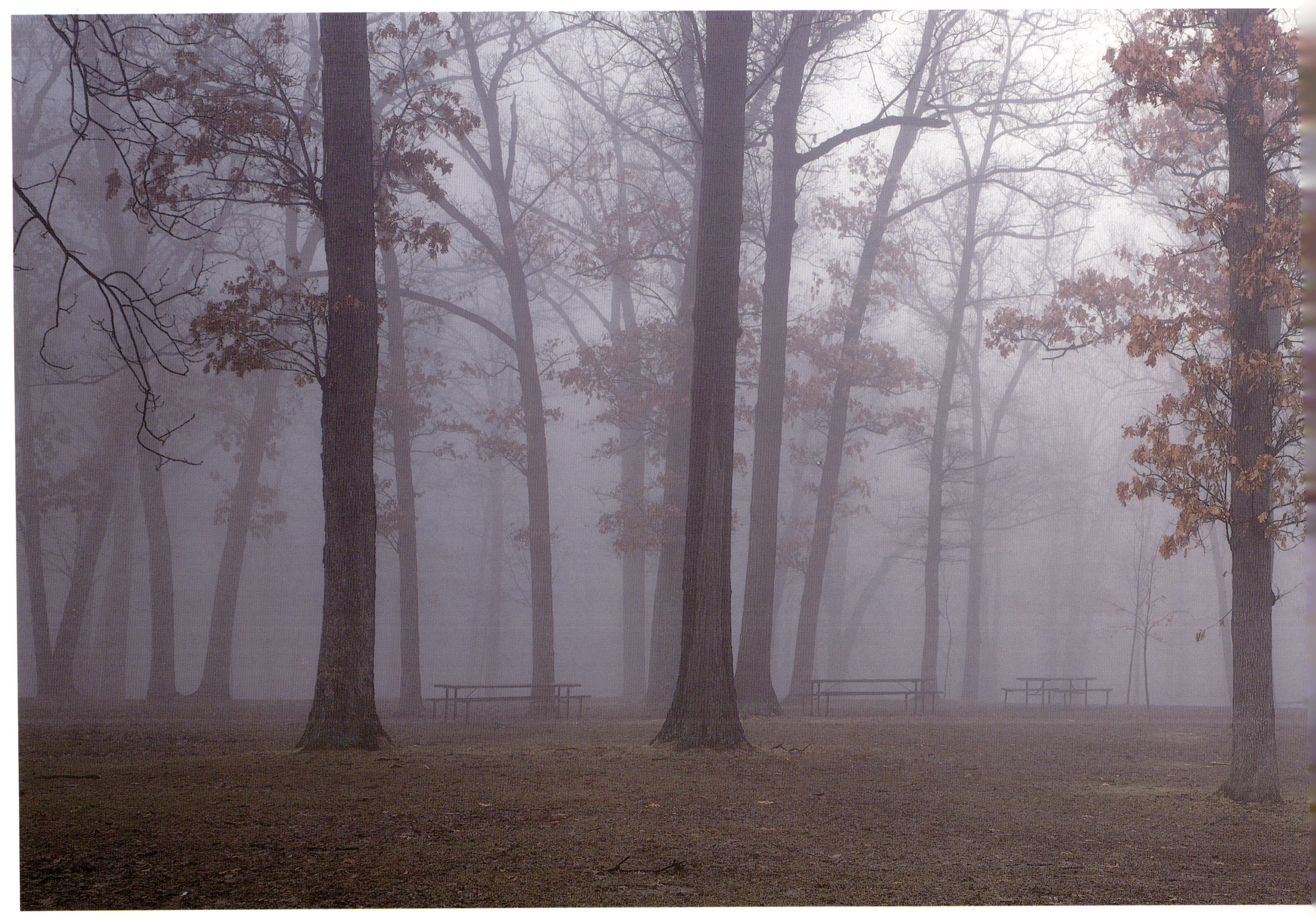

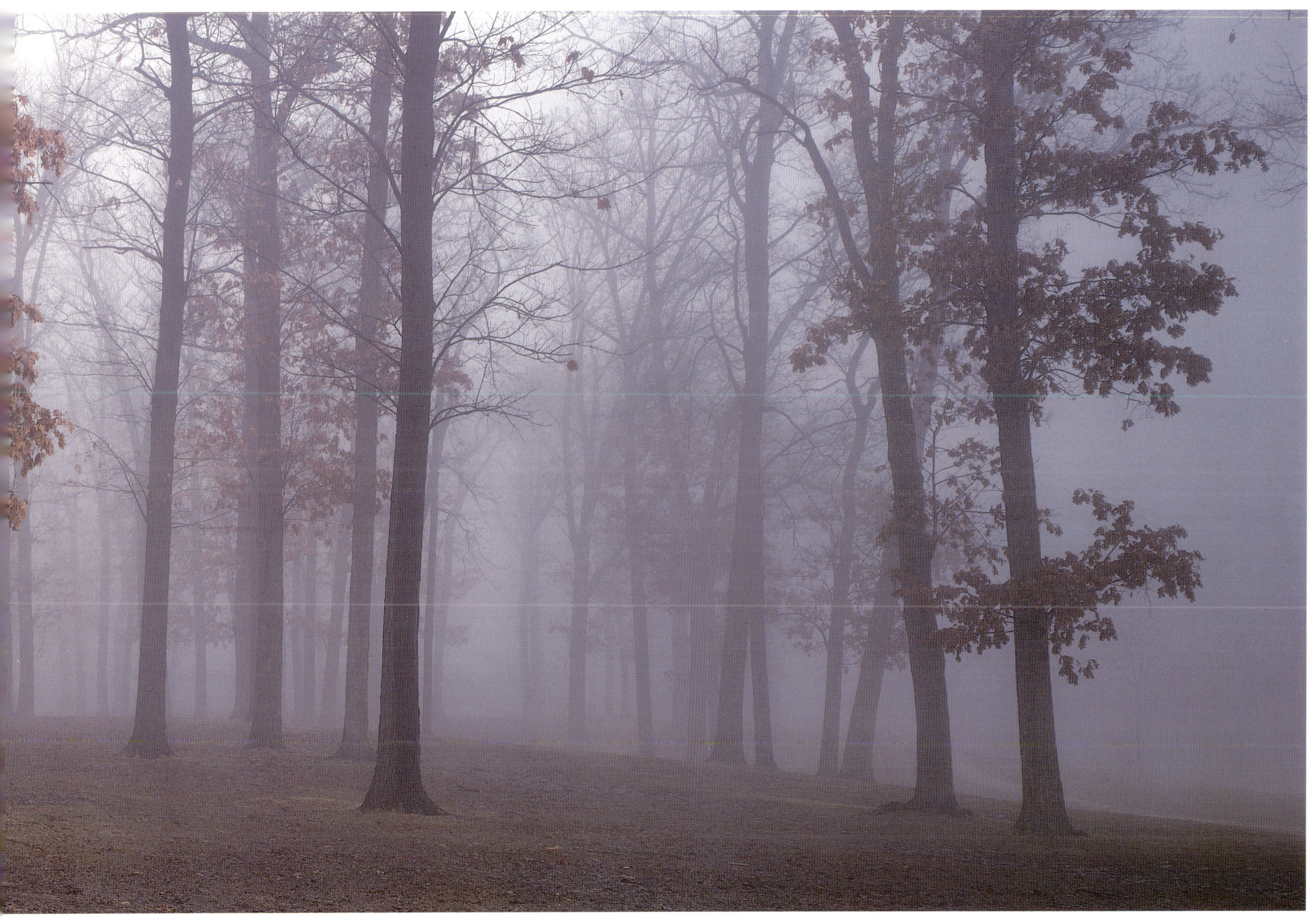

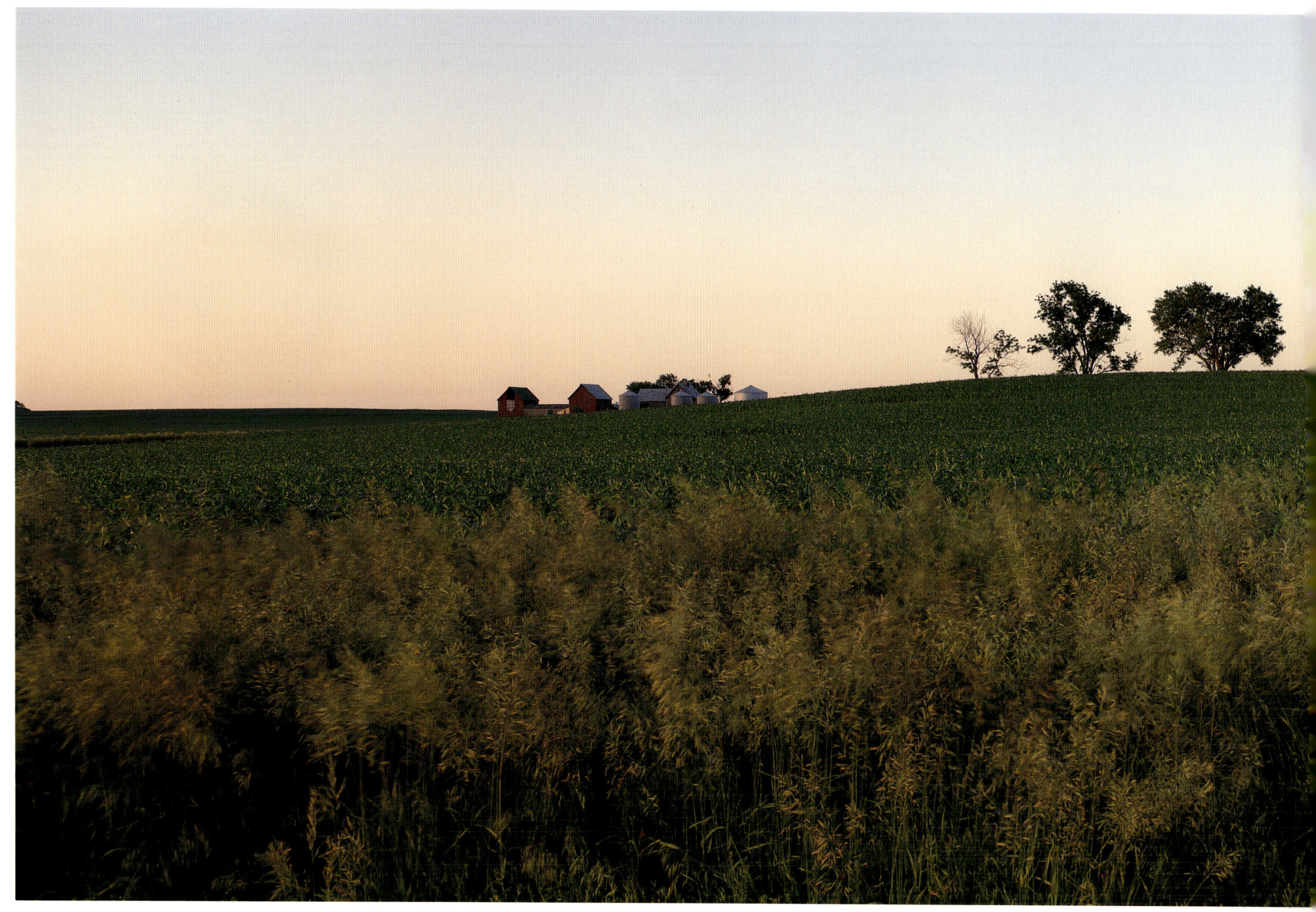

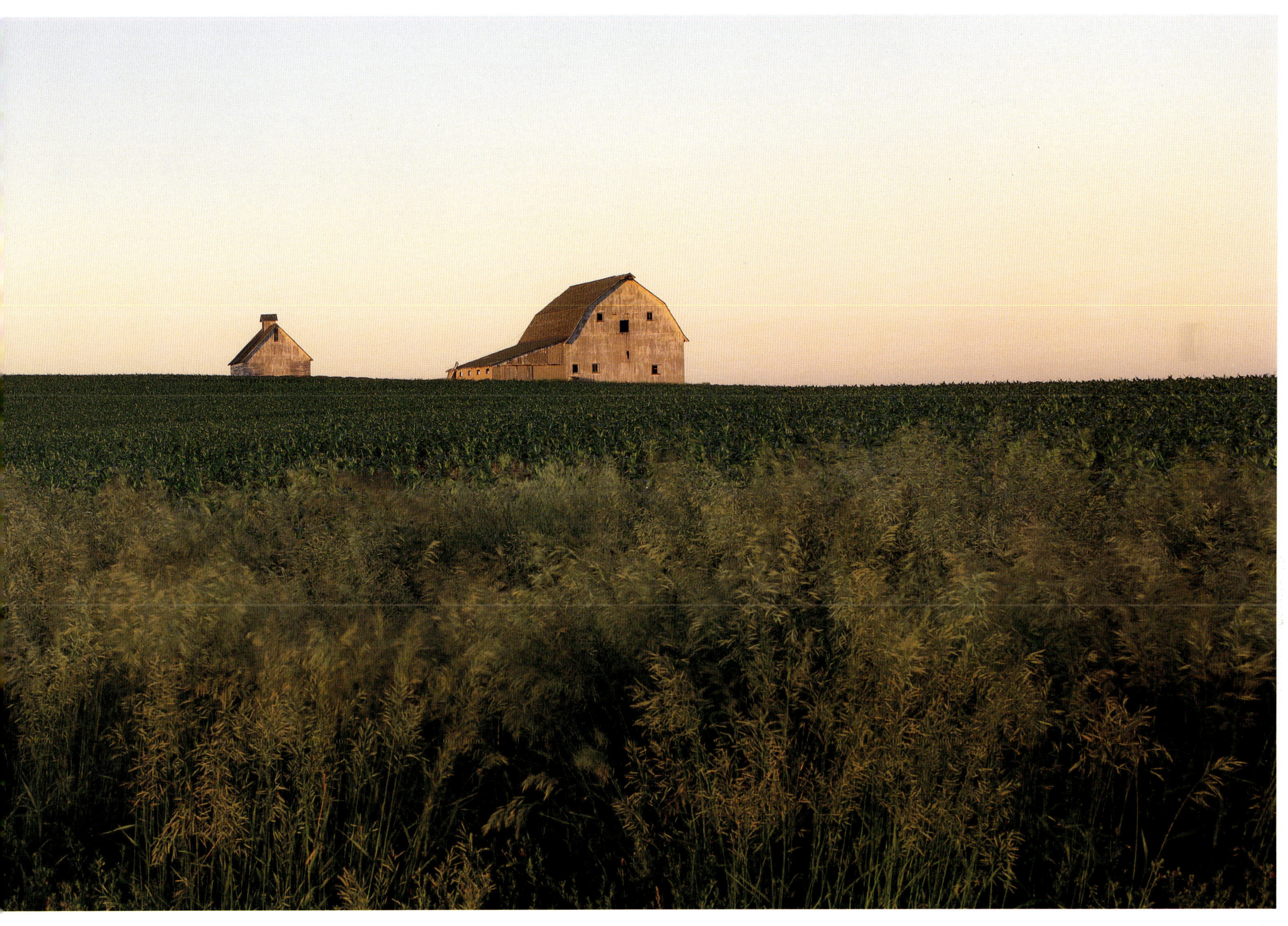

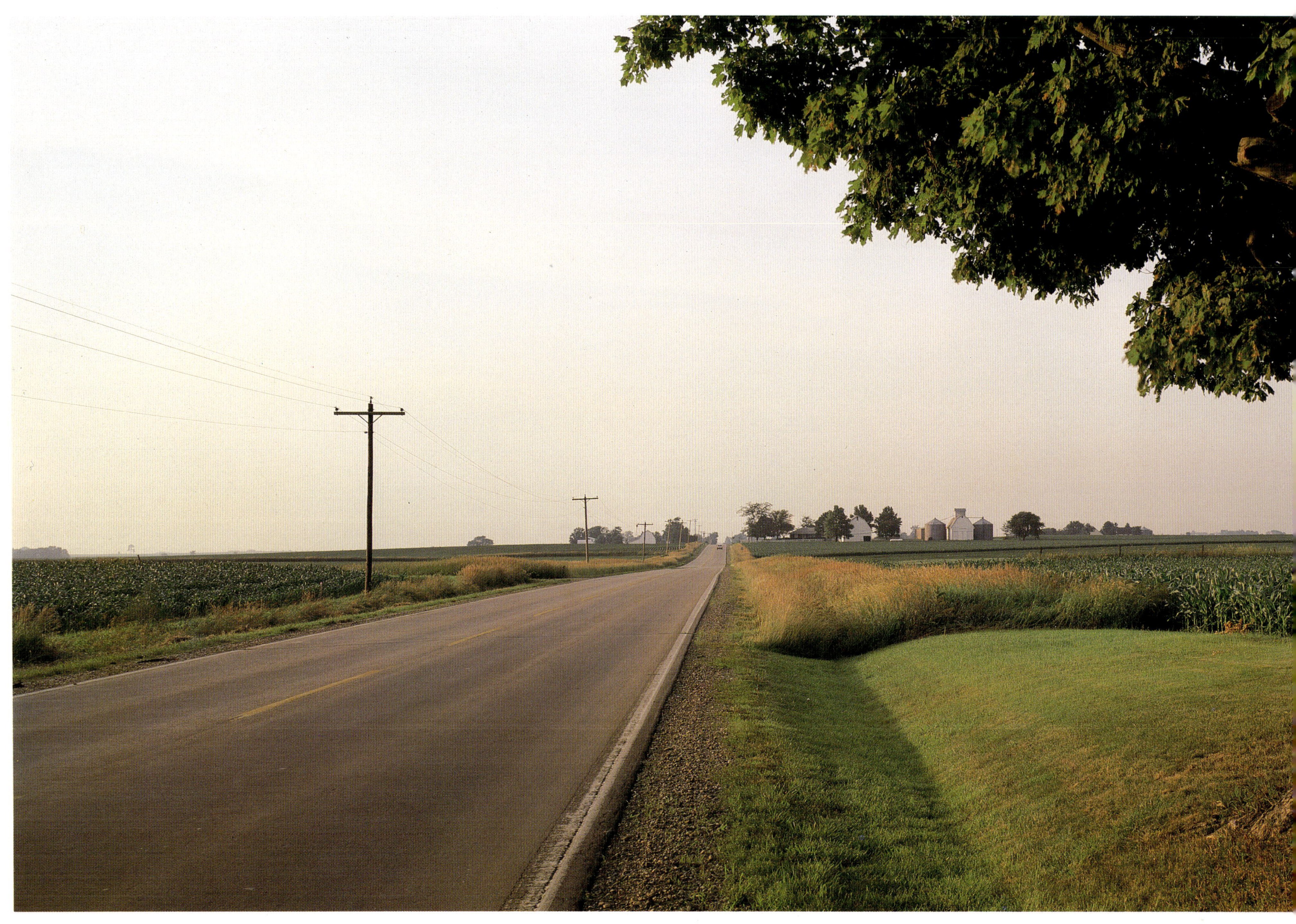

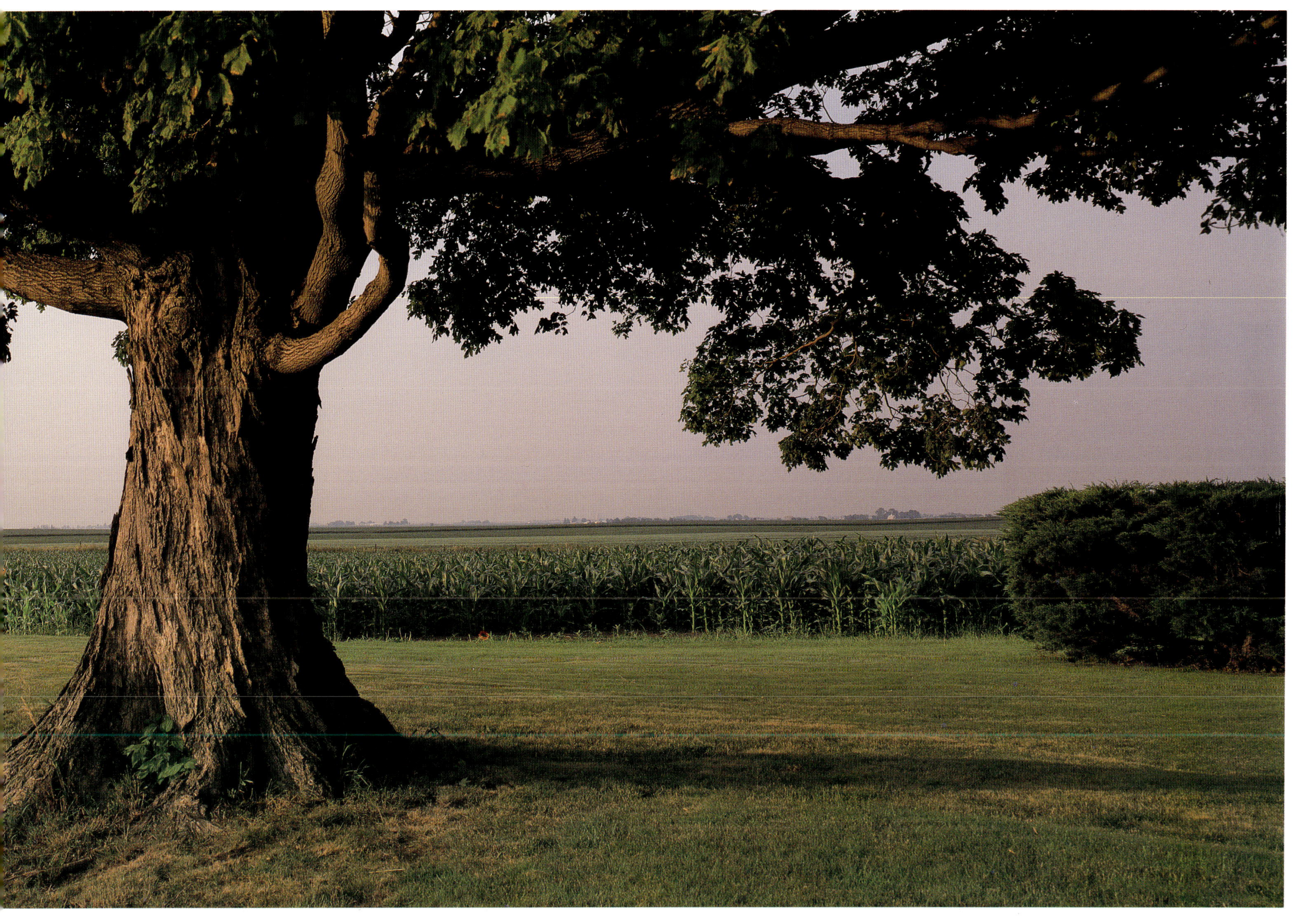

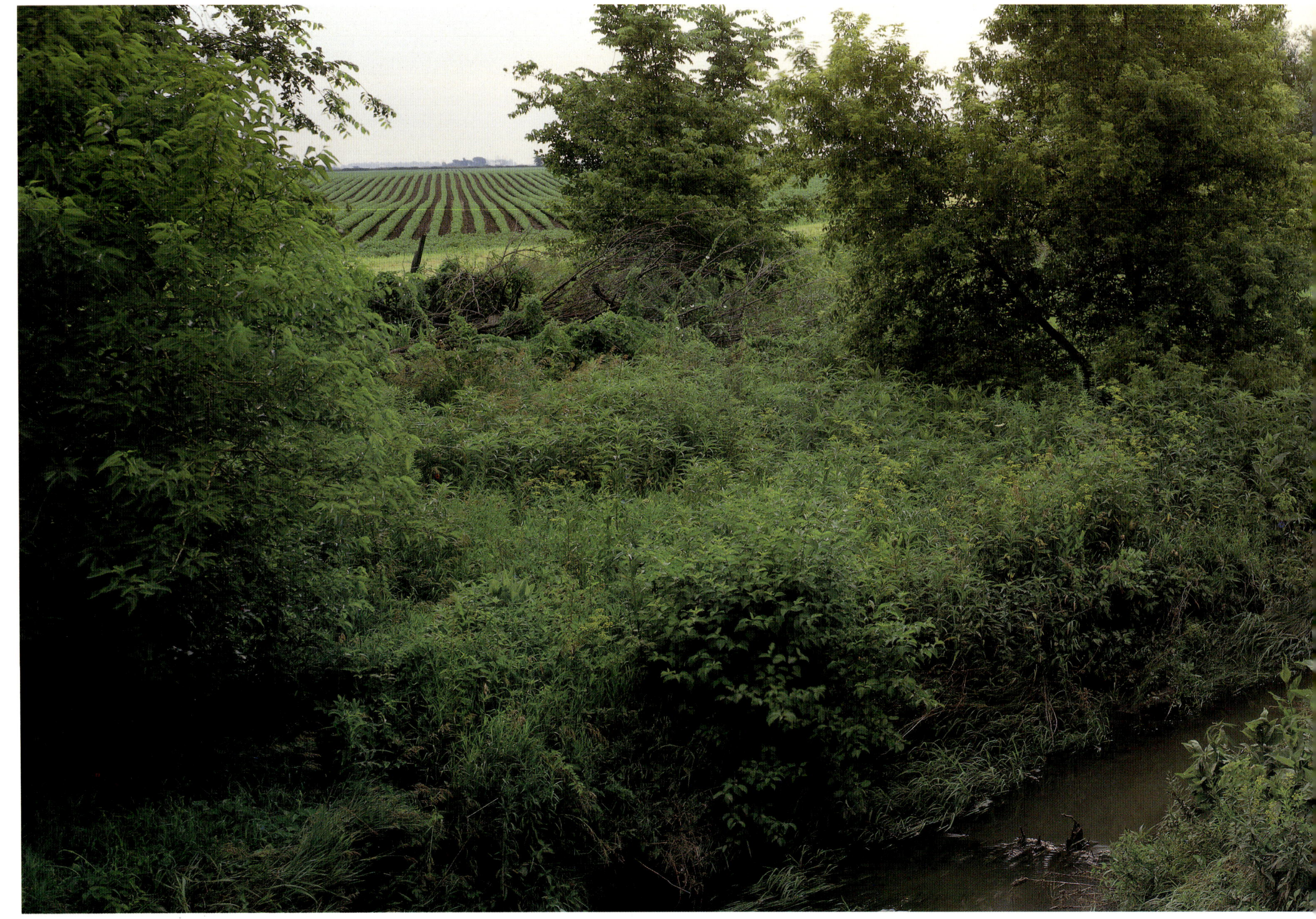

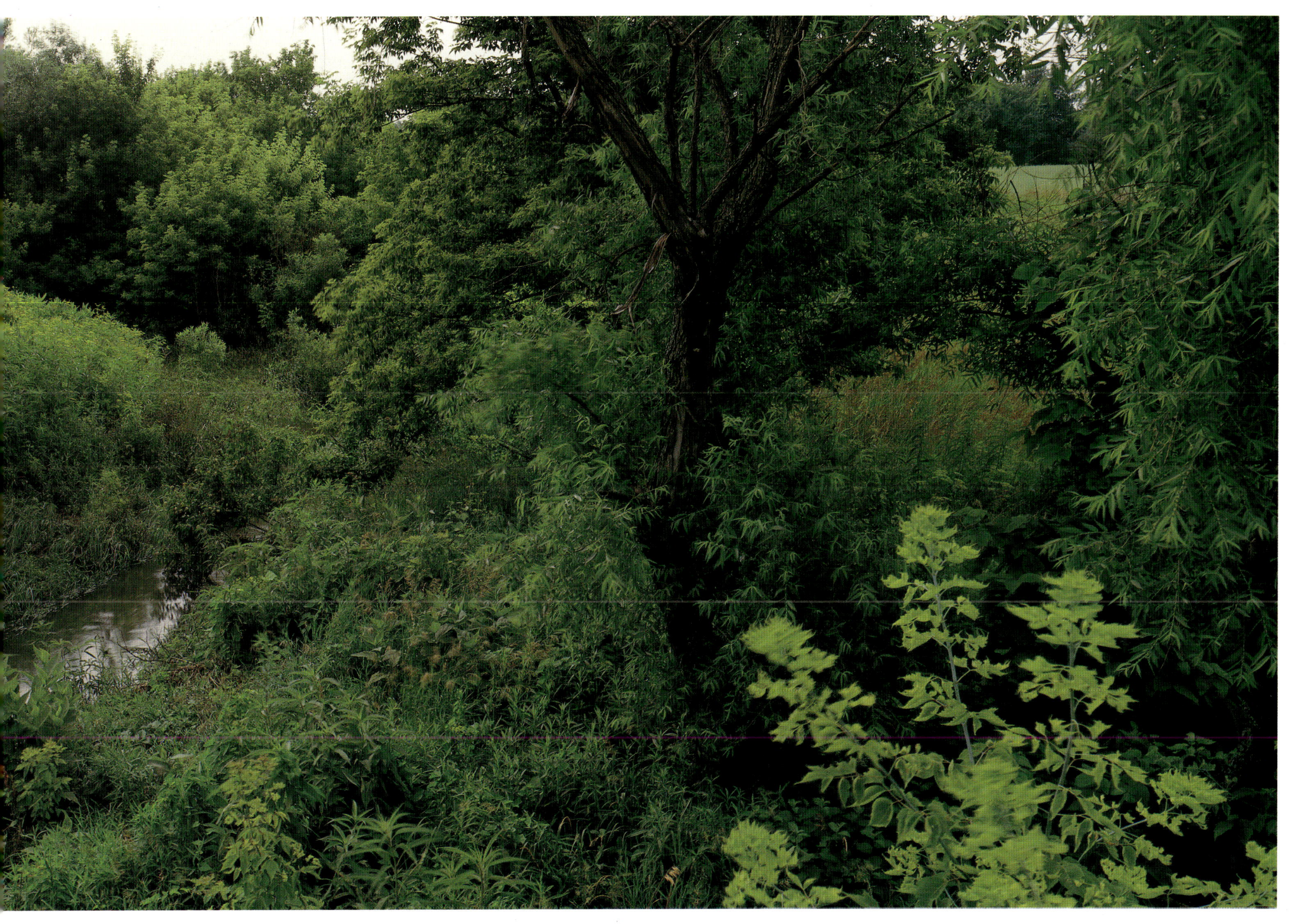

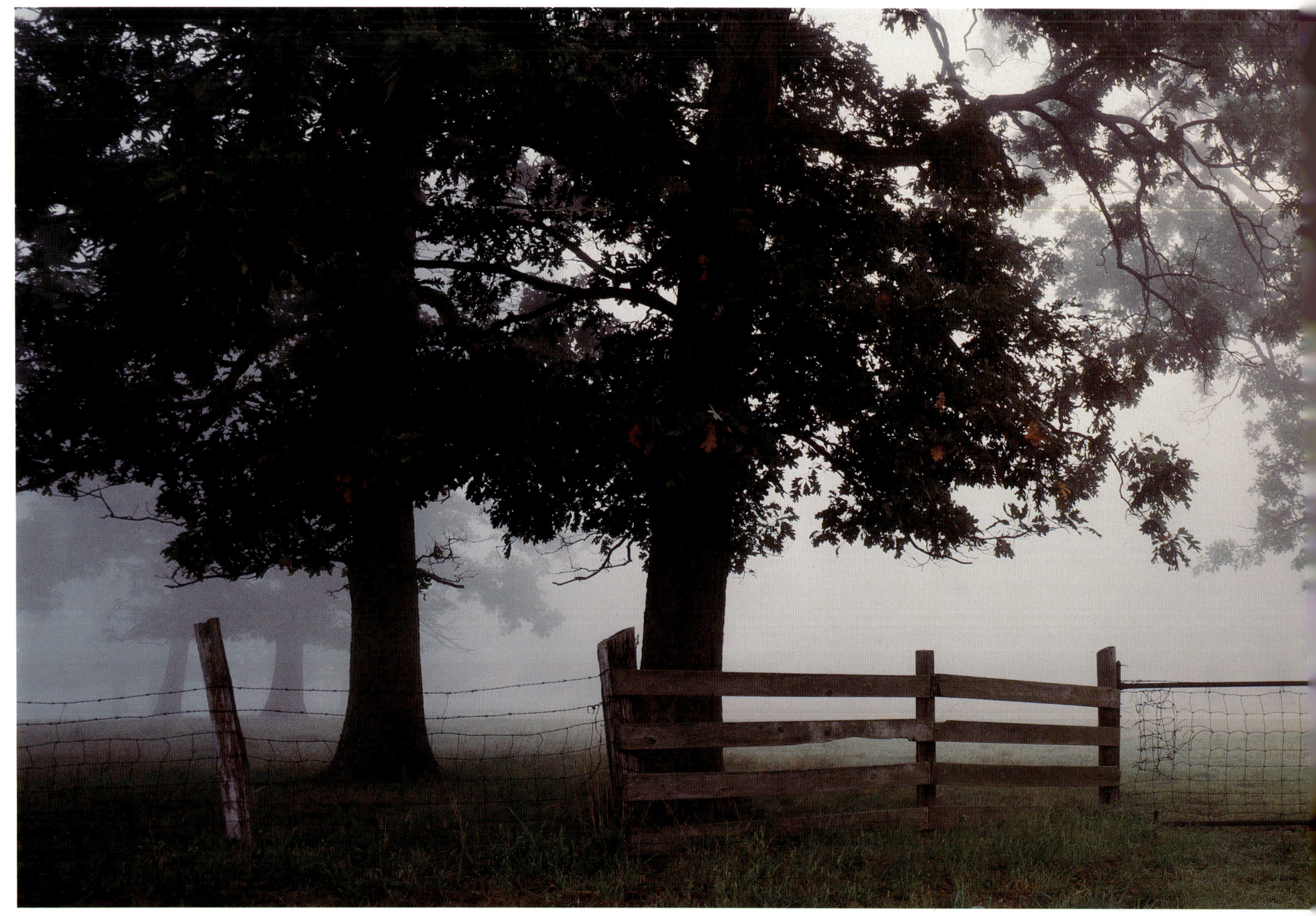

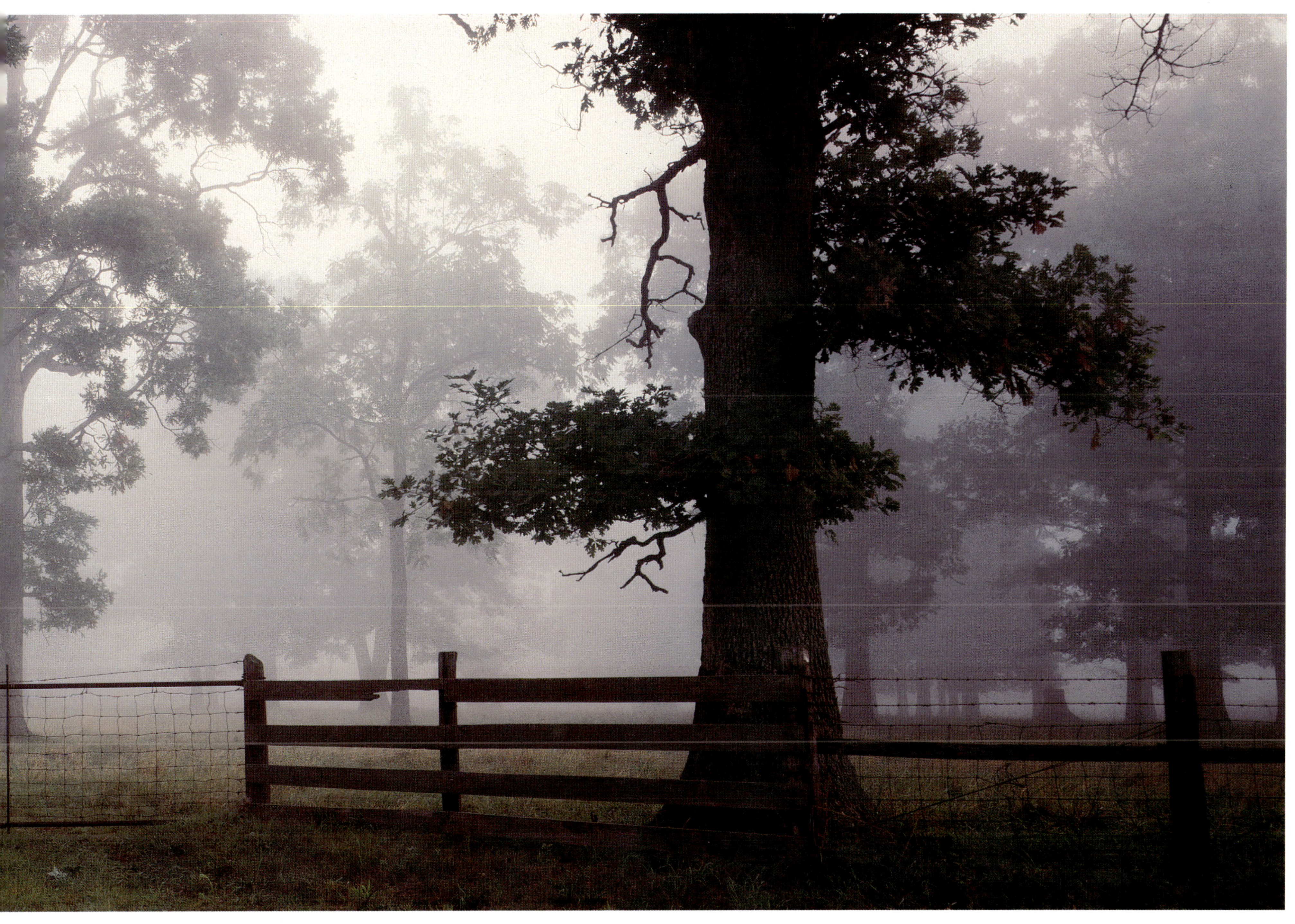

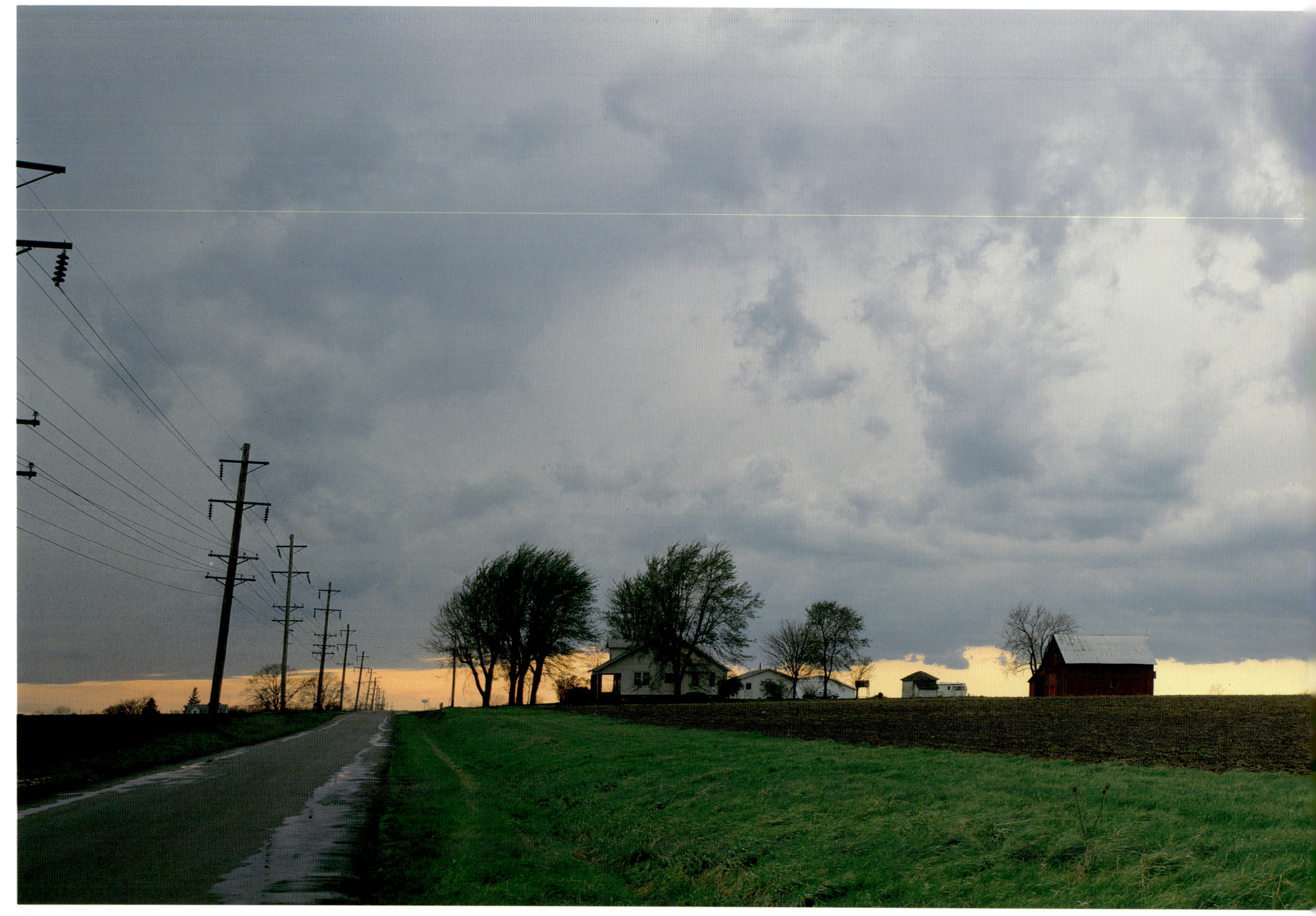

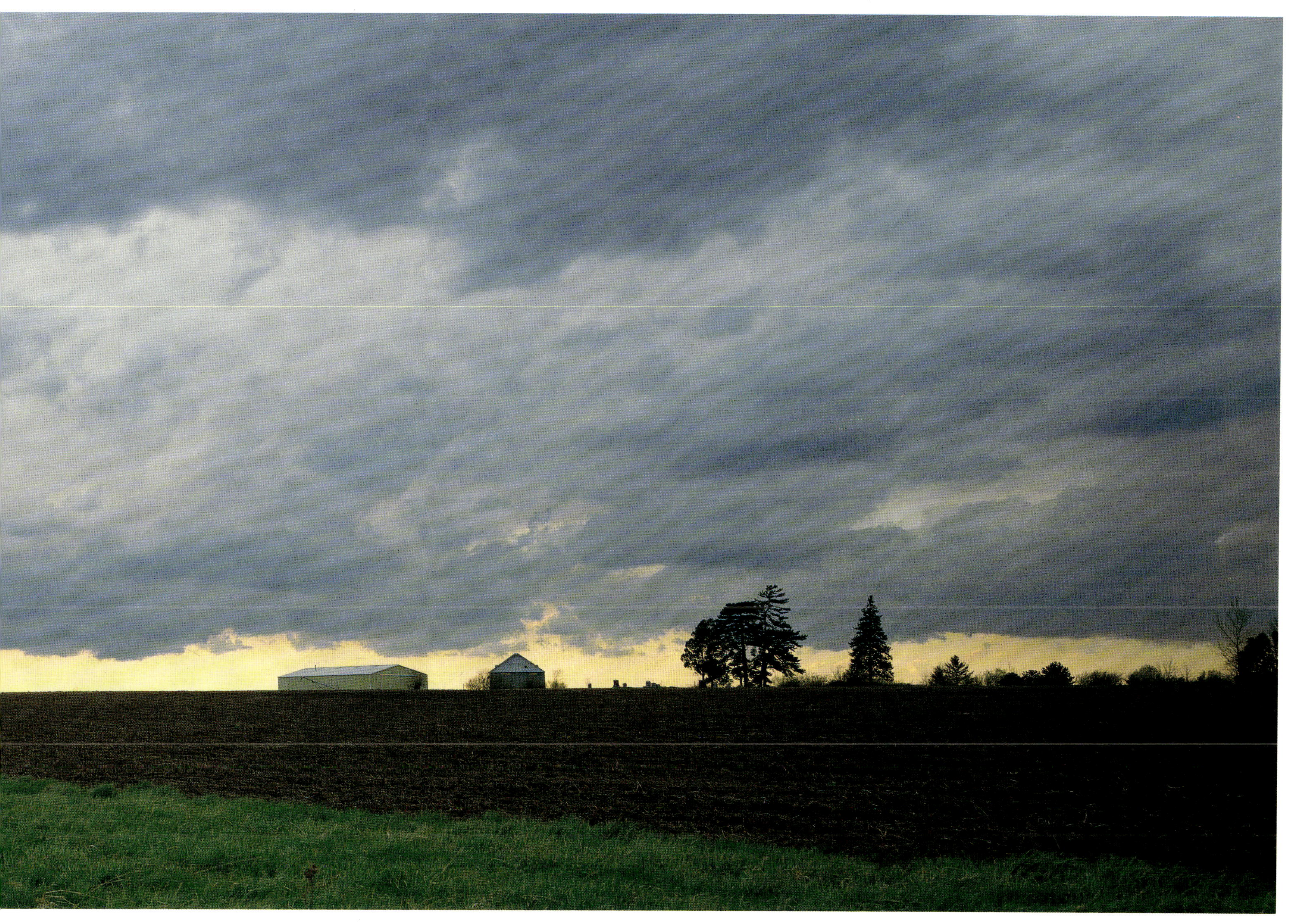

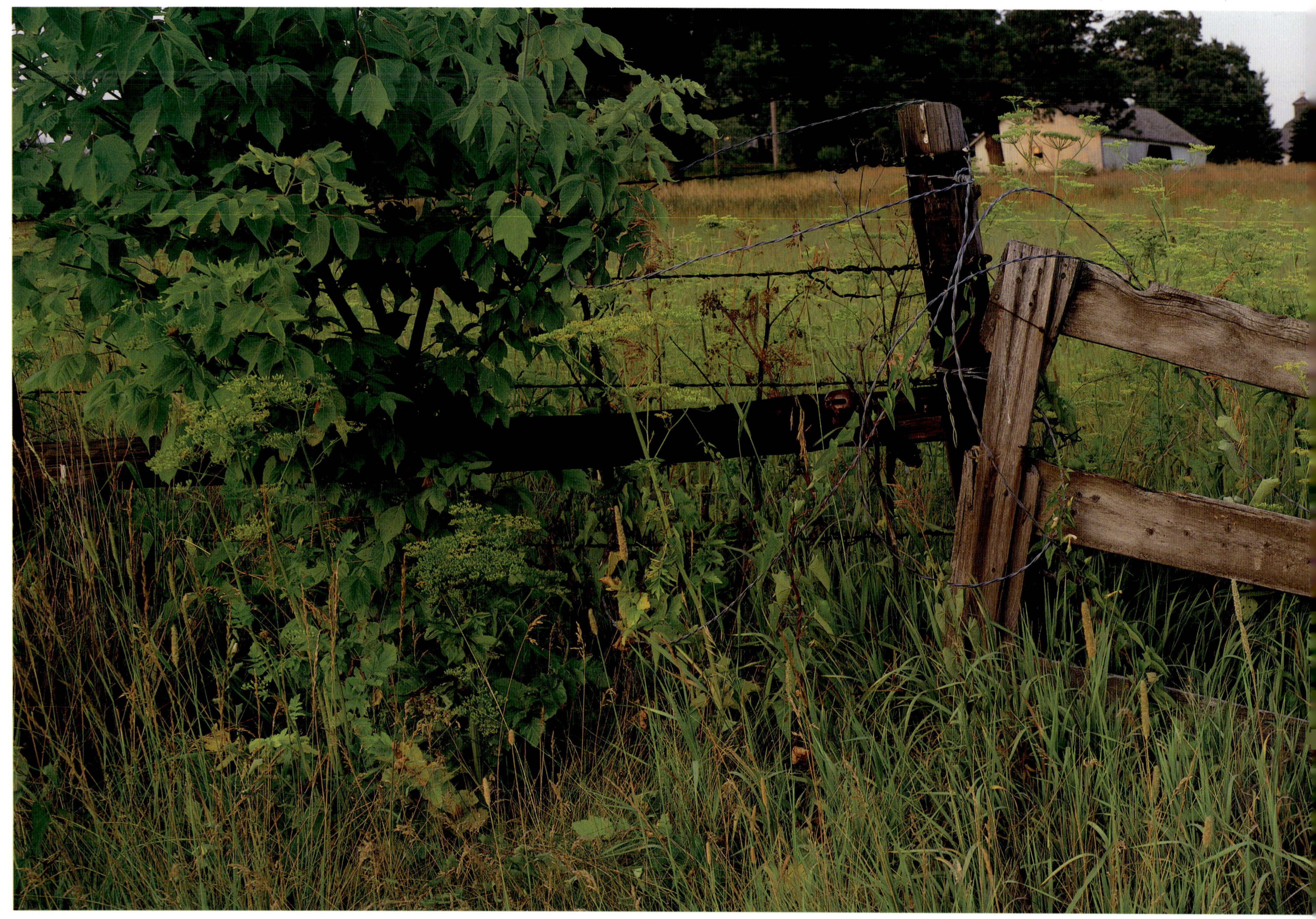

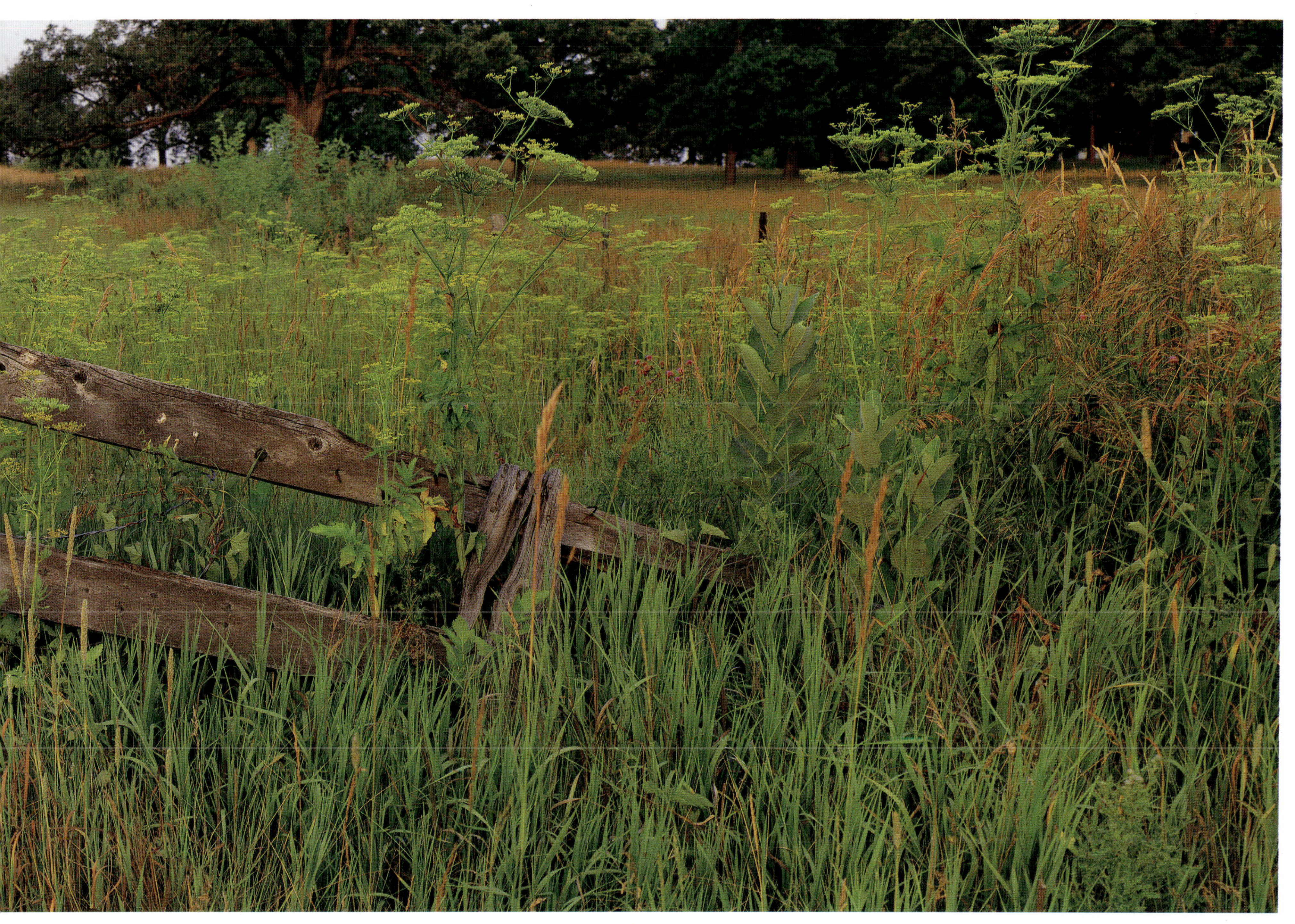

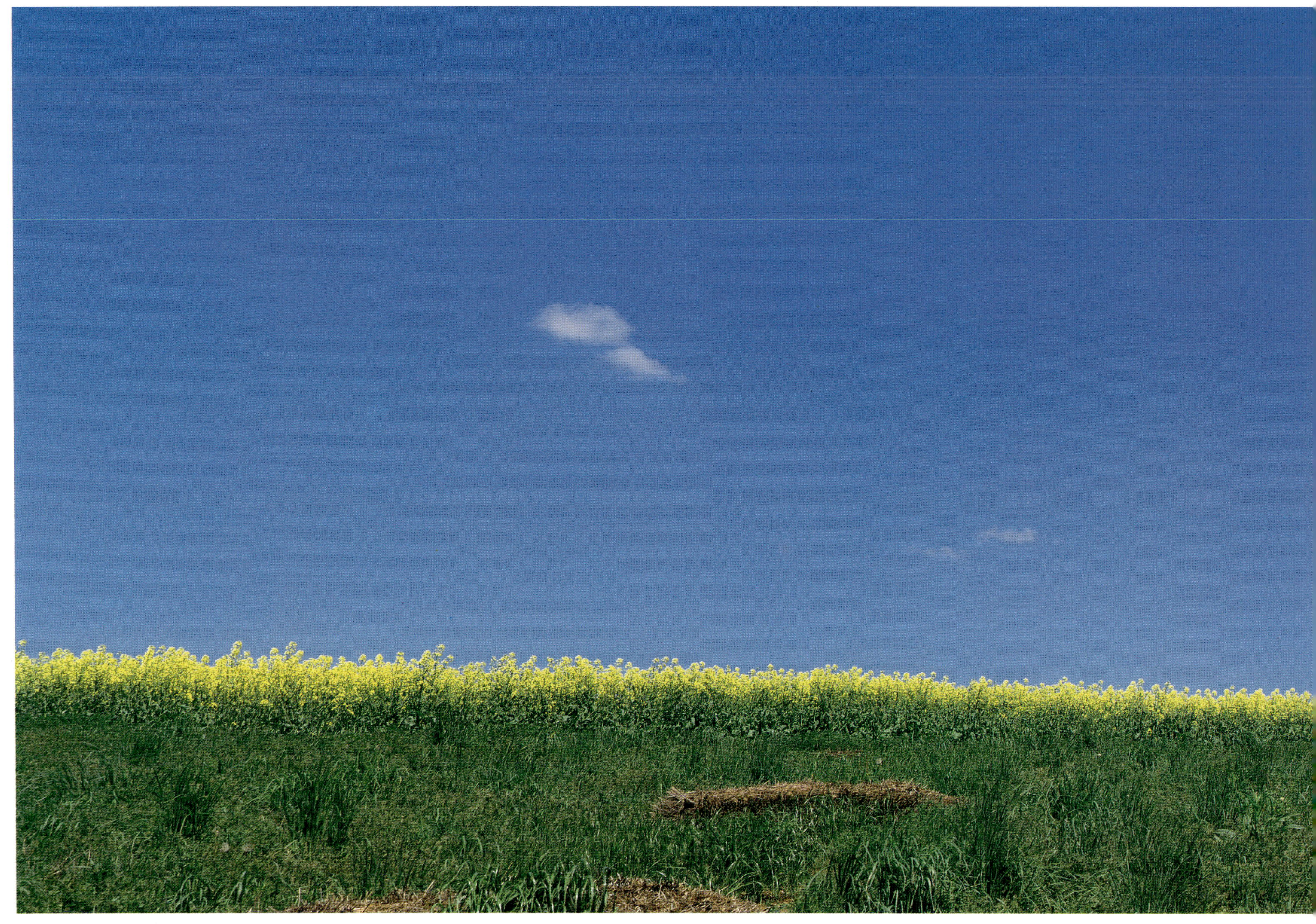

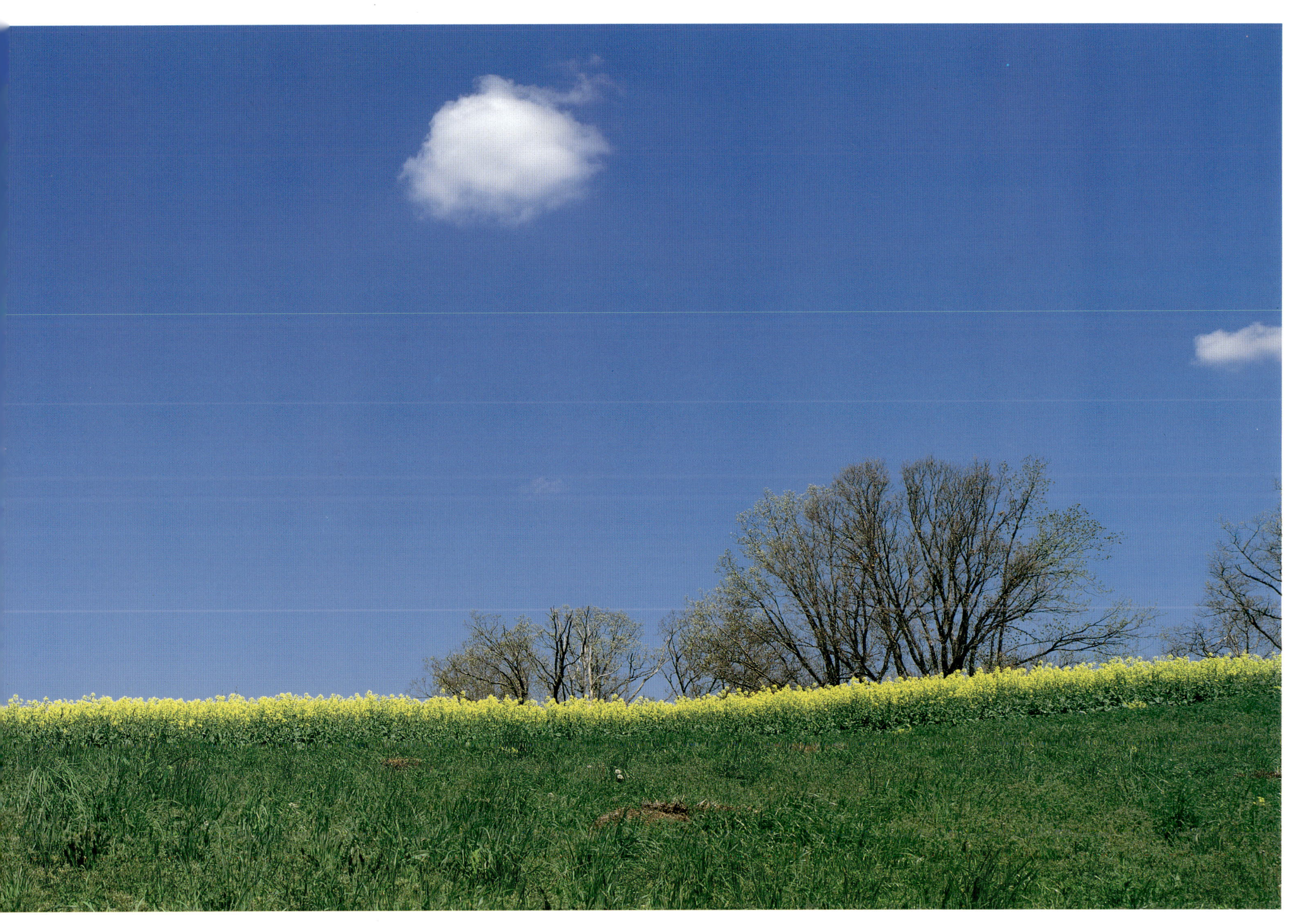

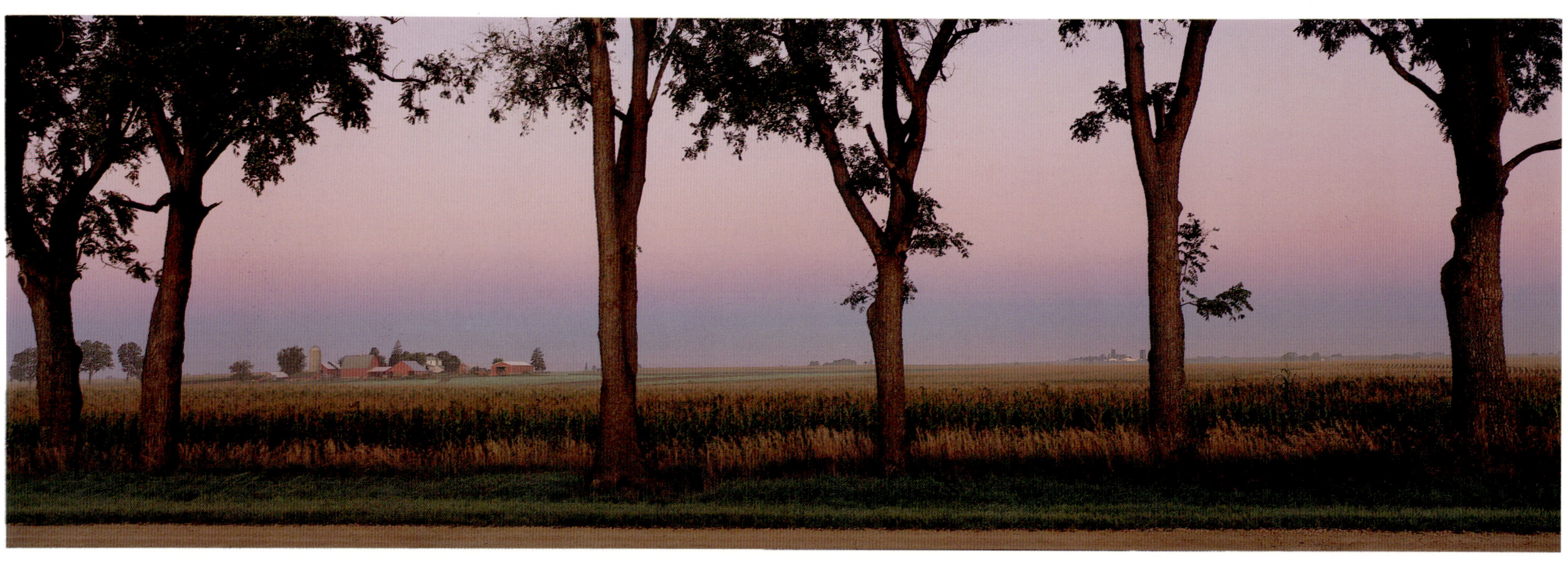

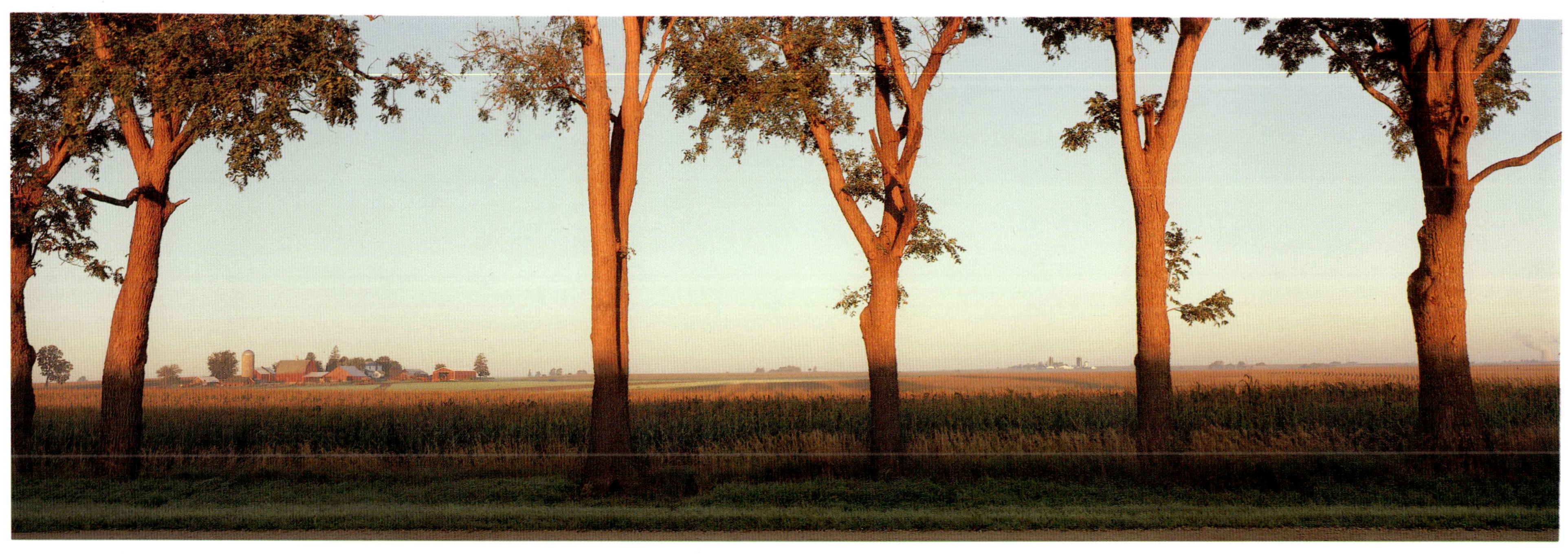

19

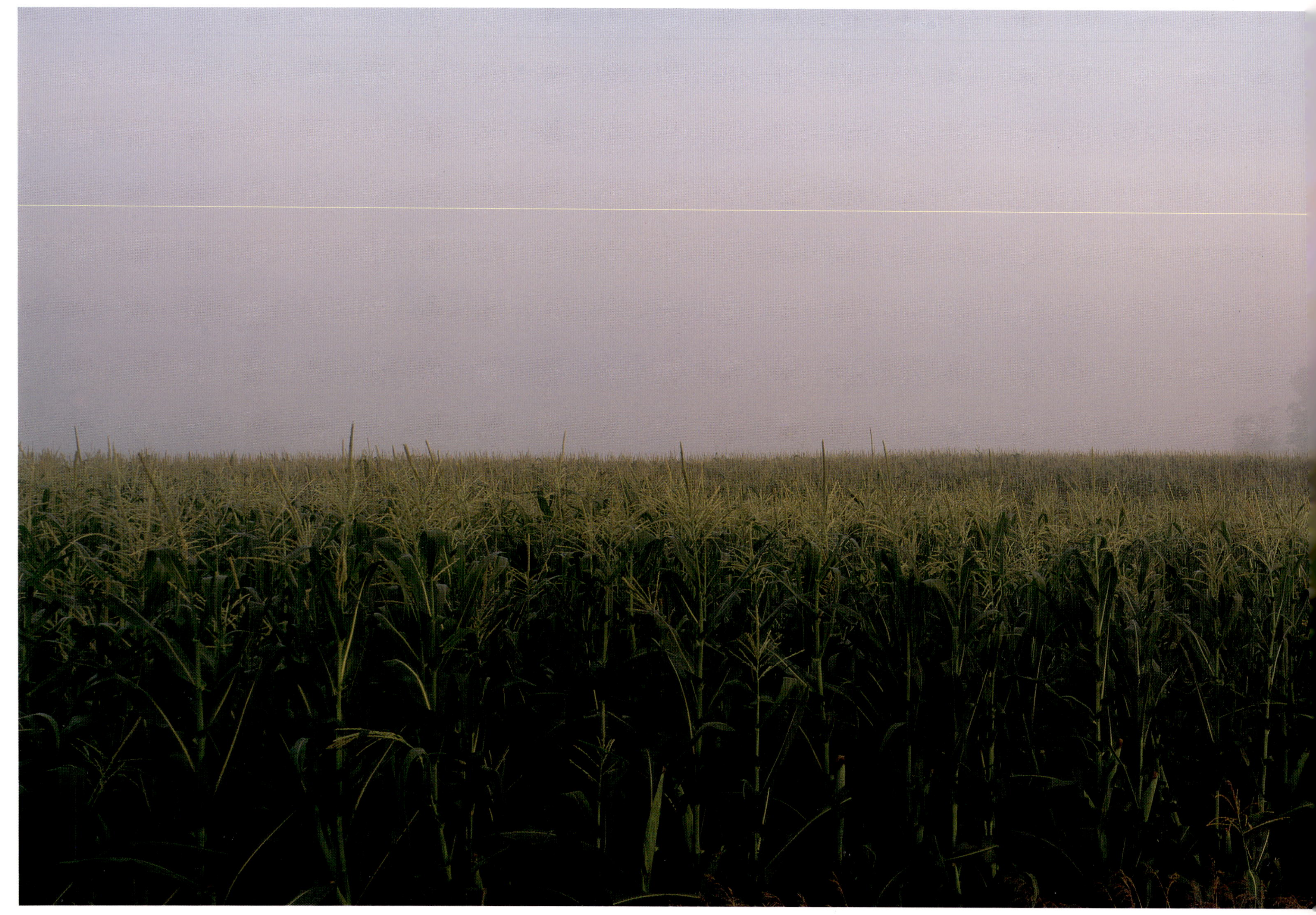

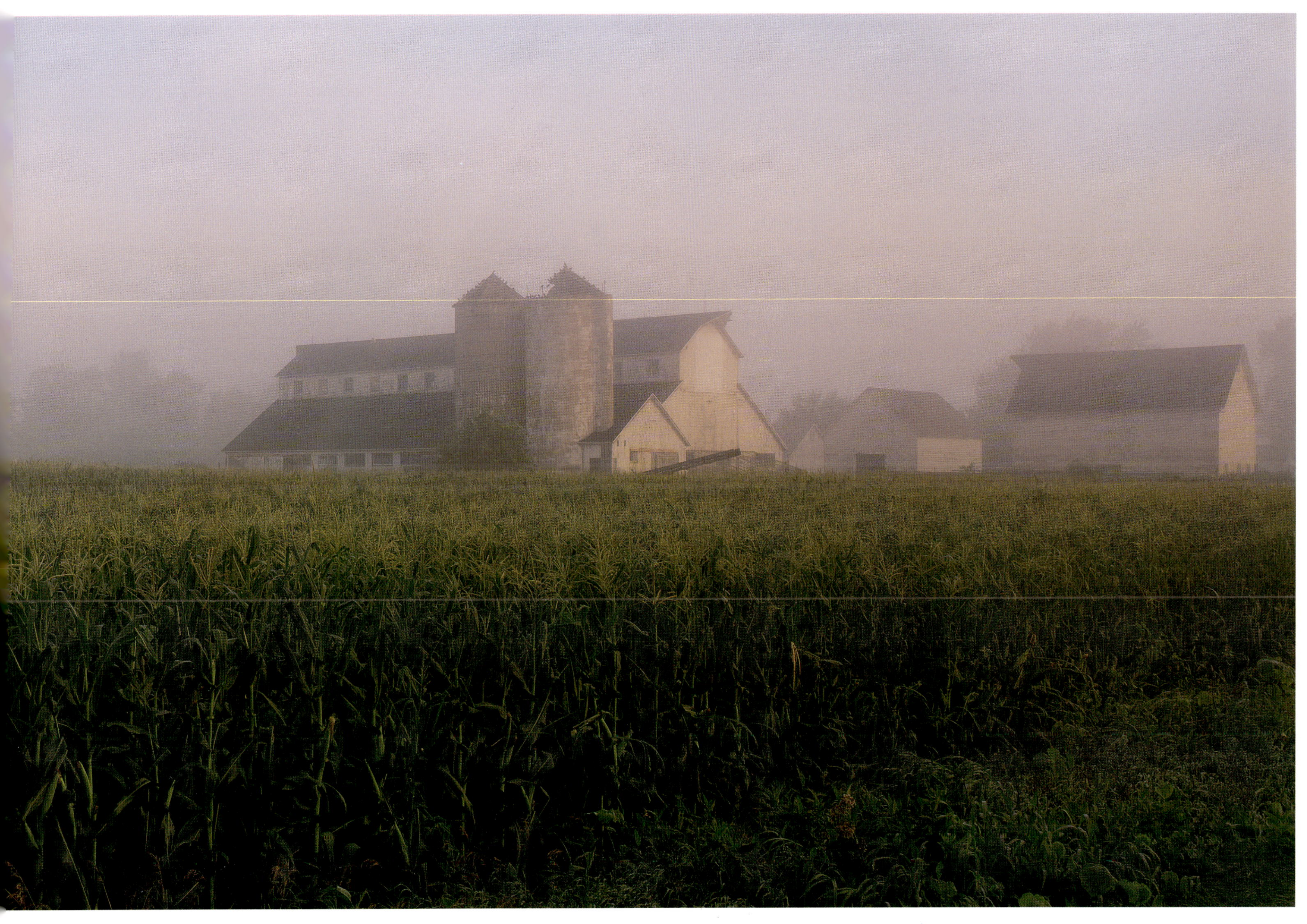

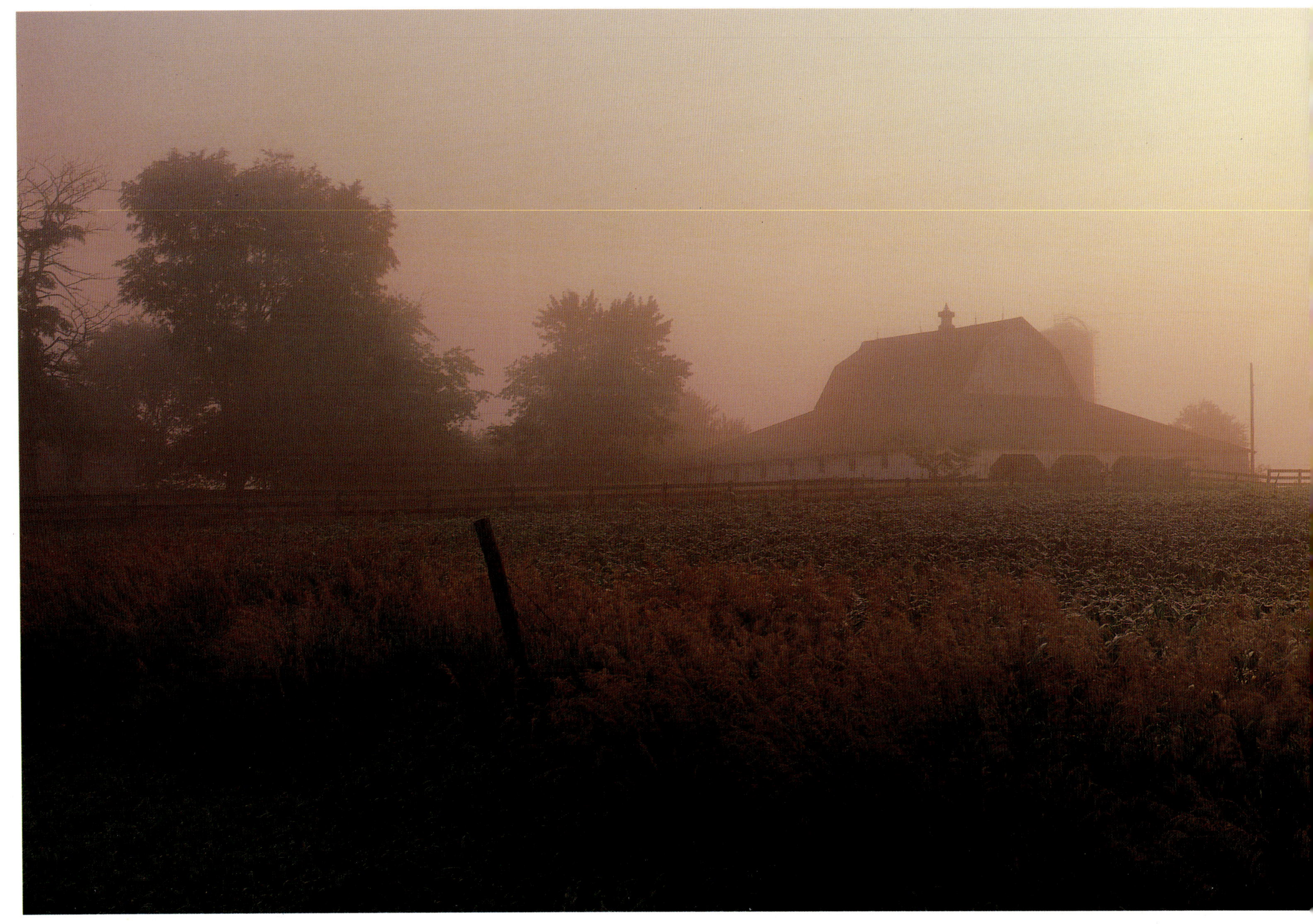

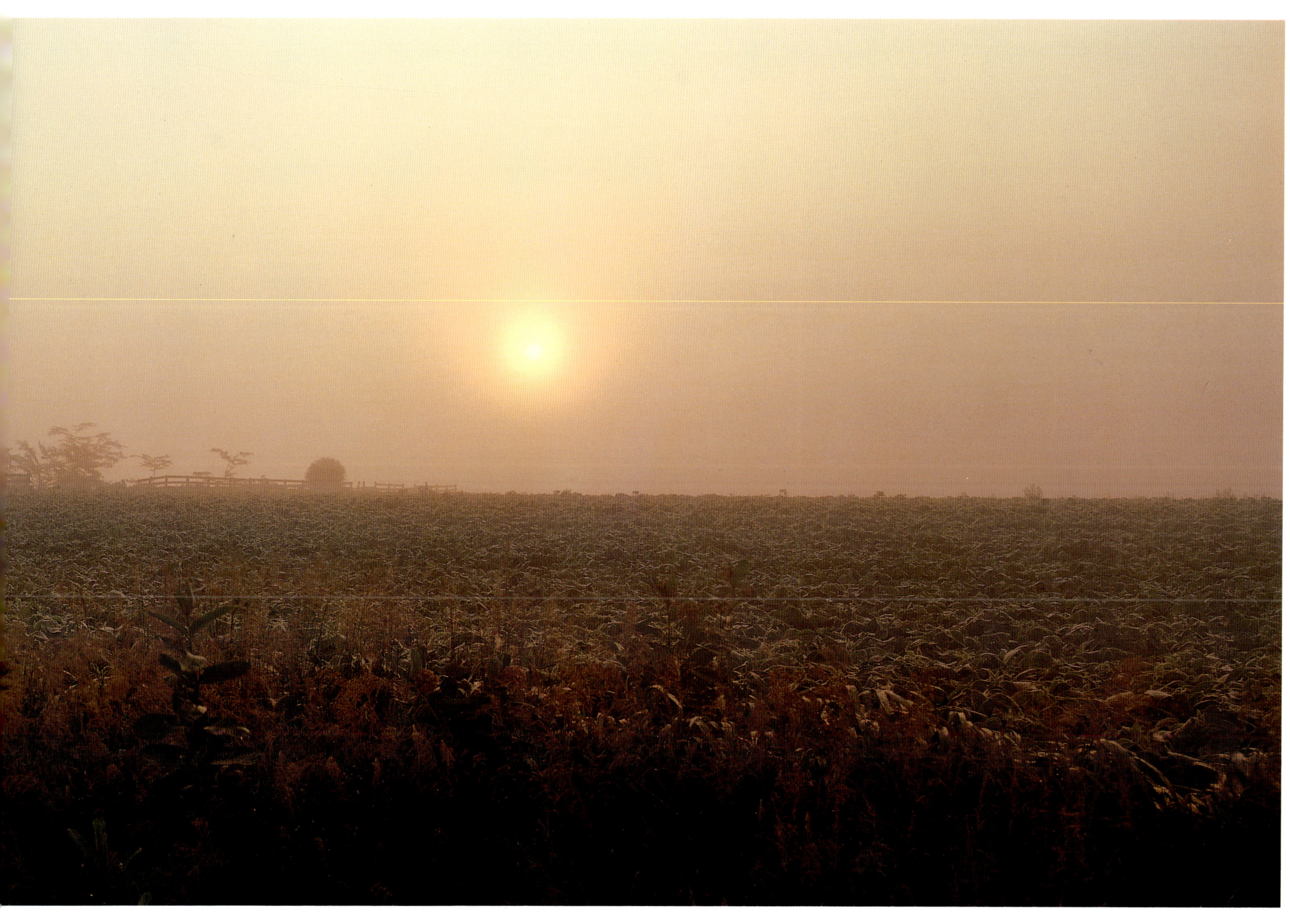

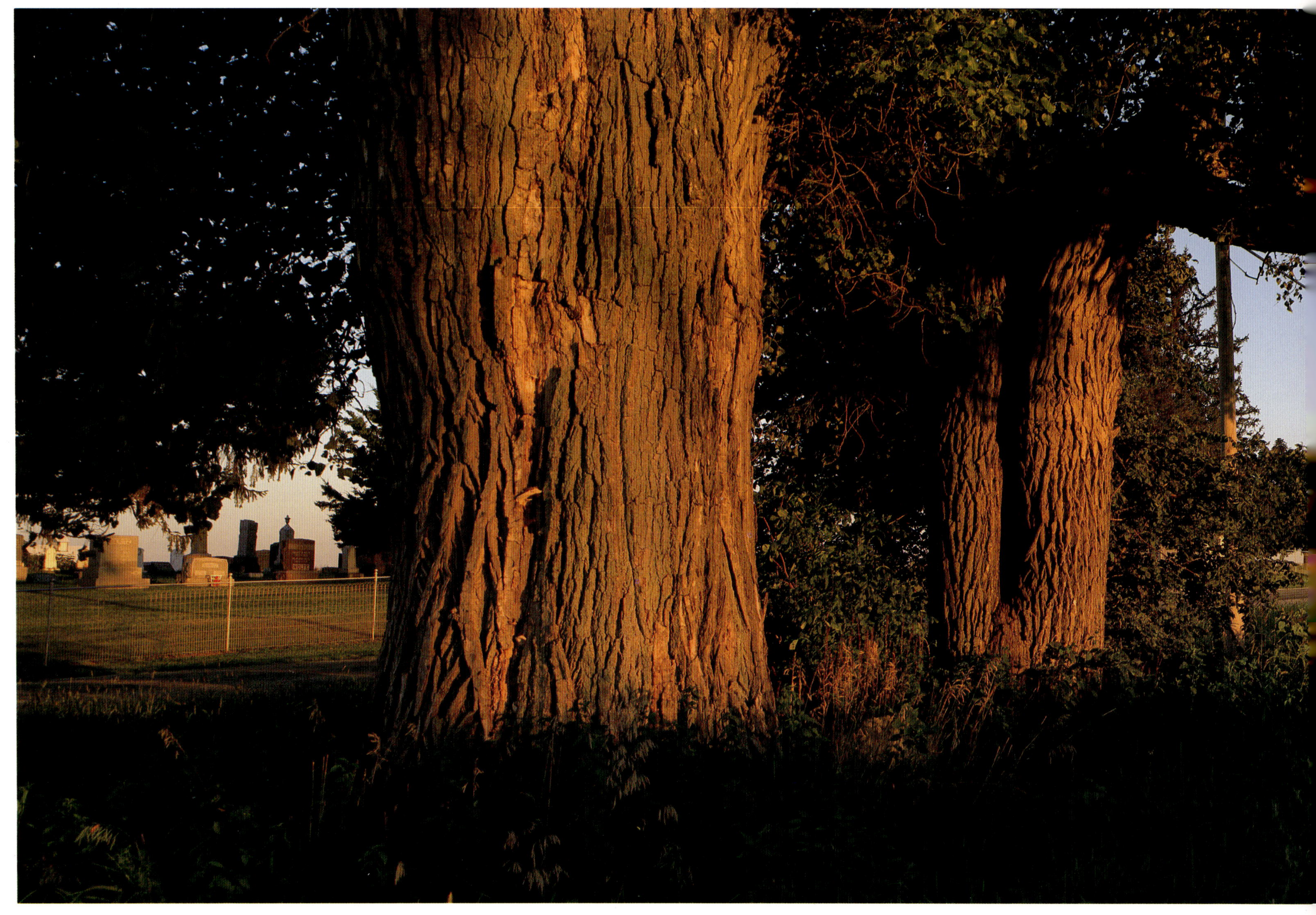

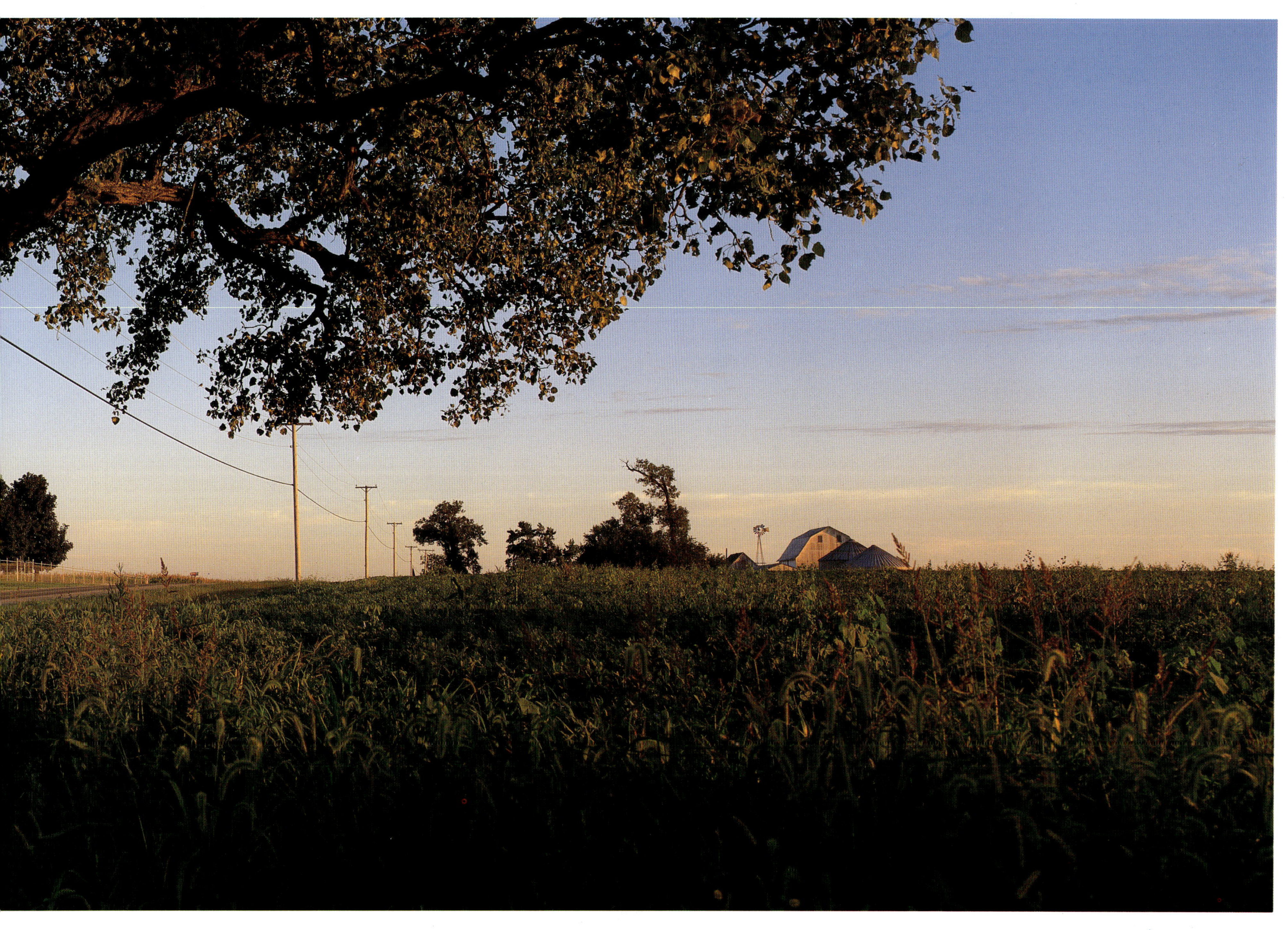

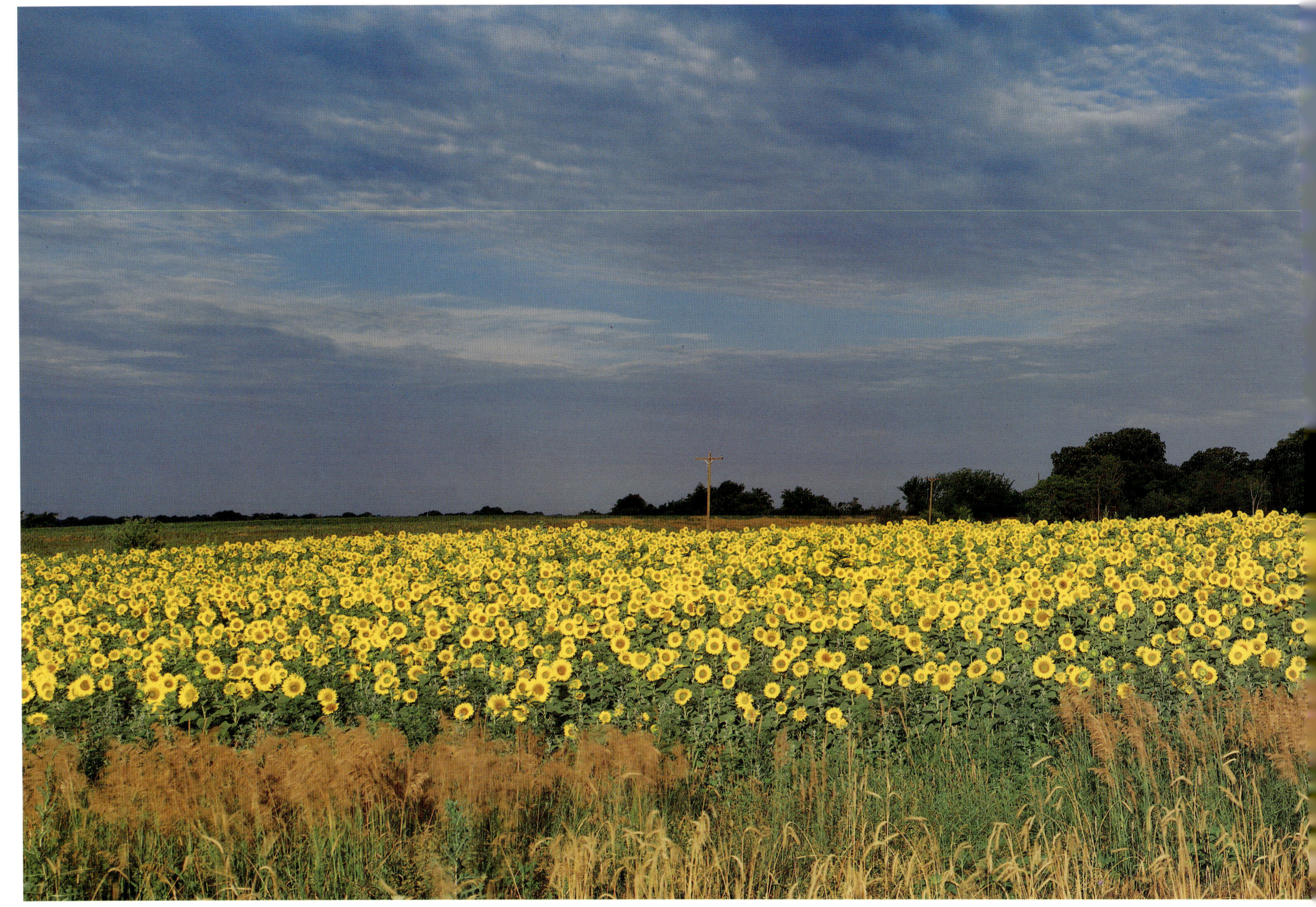

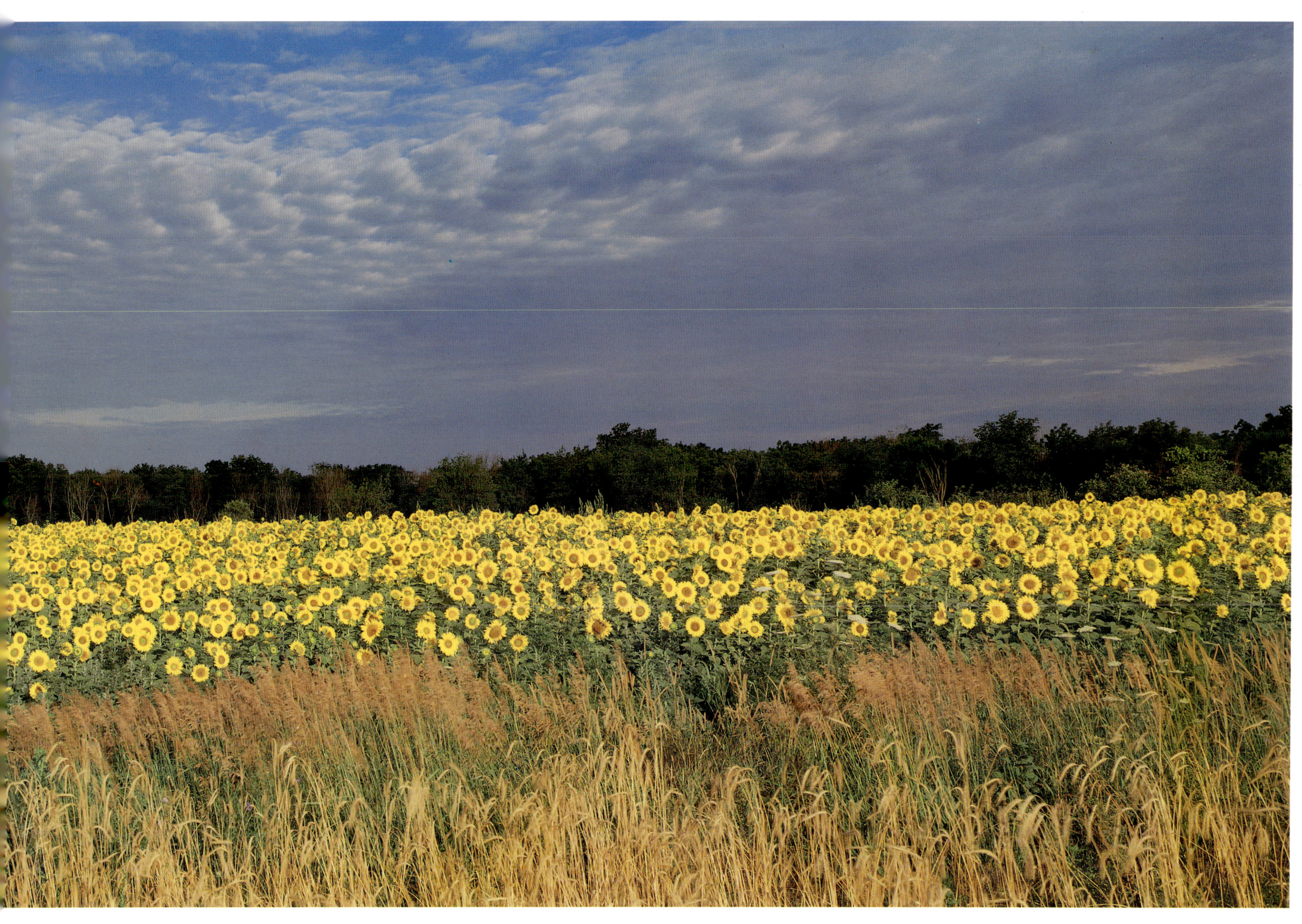

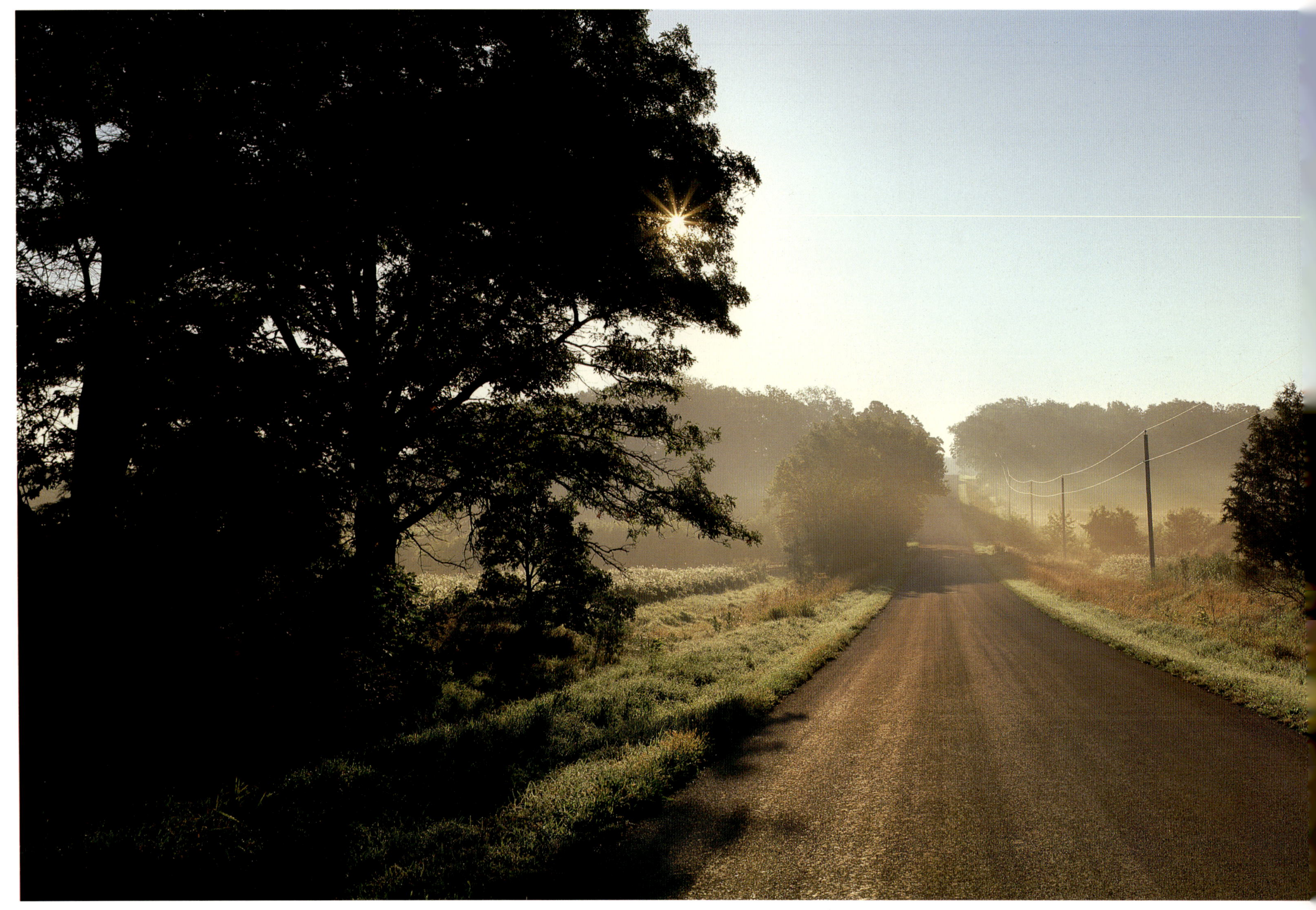

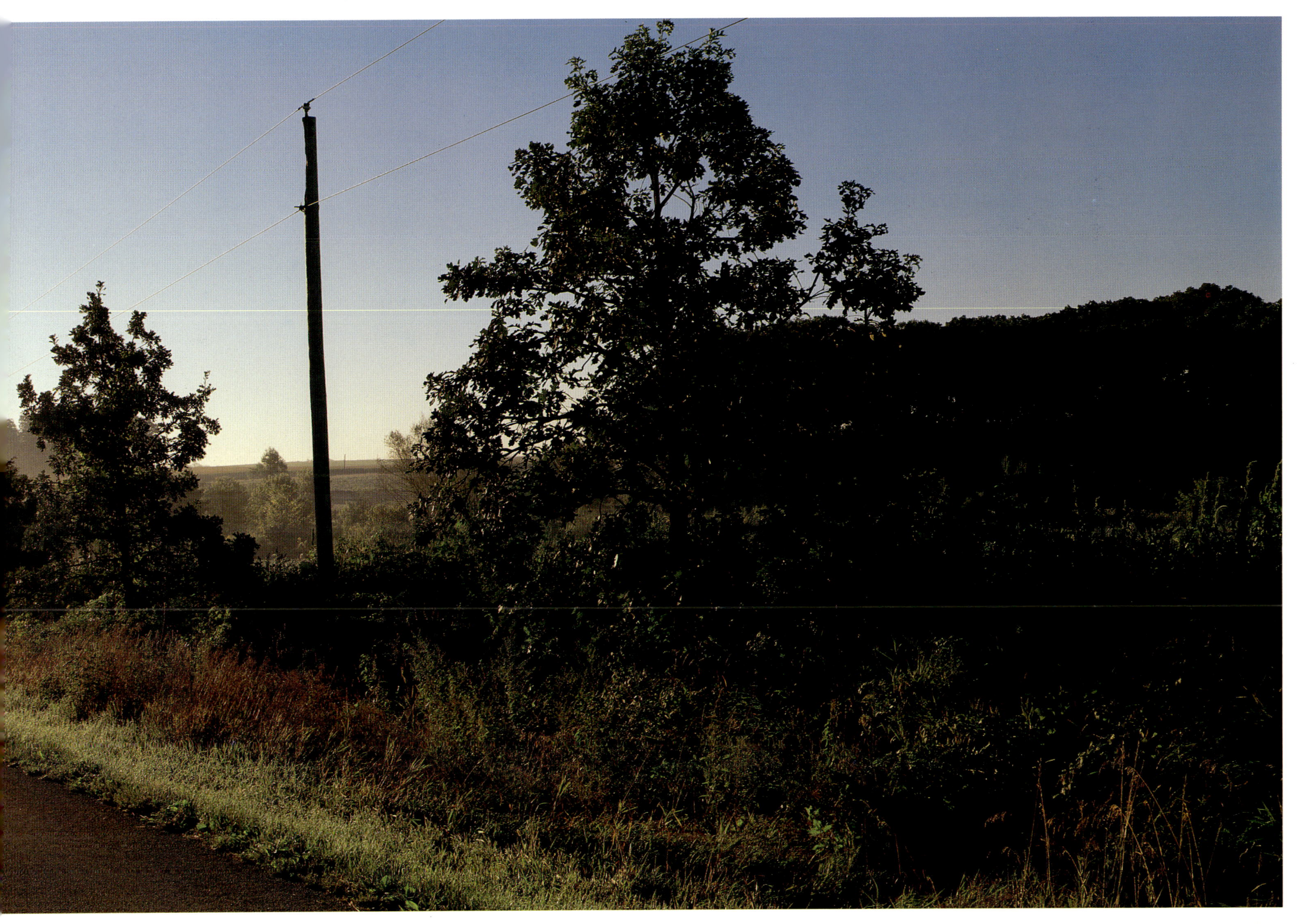

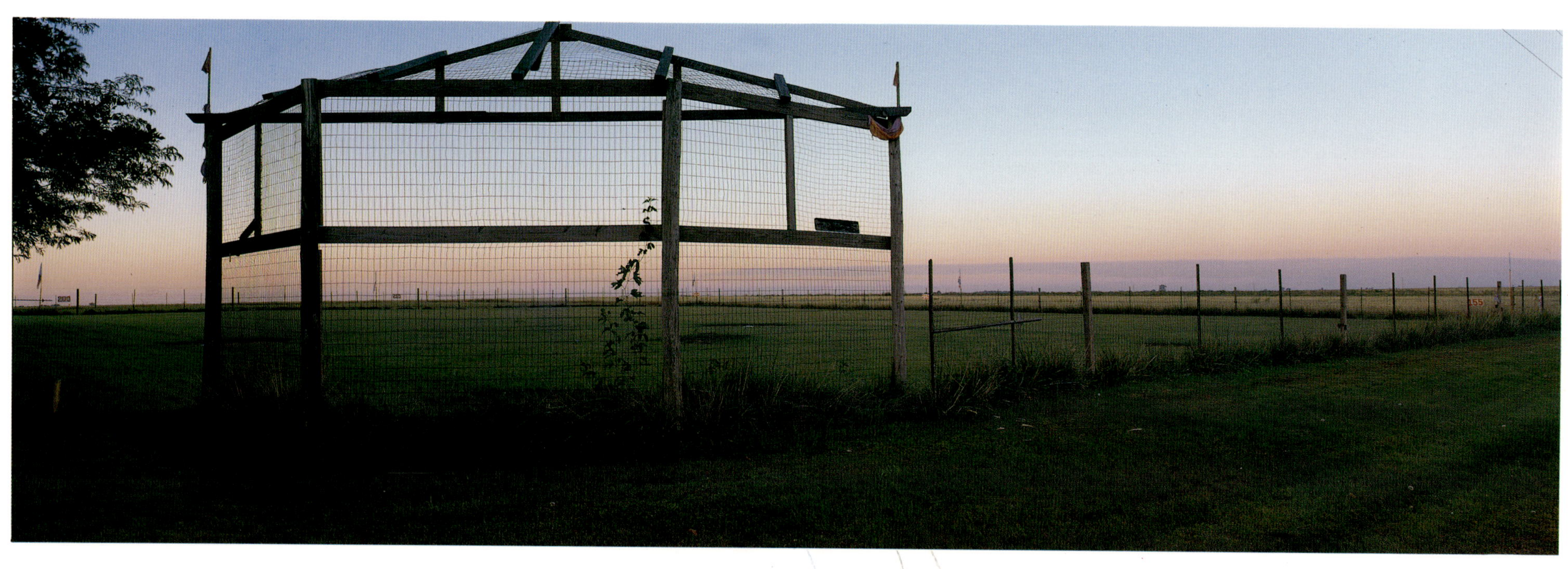

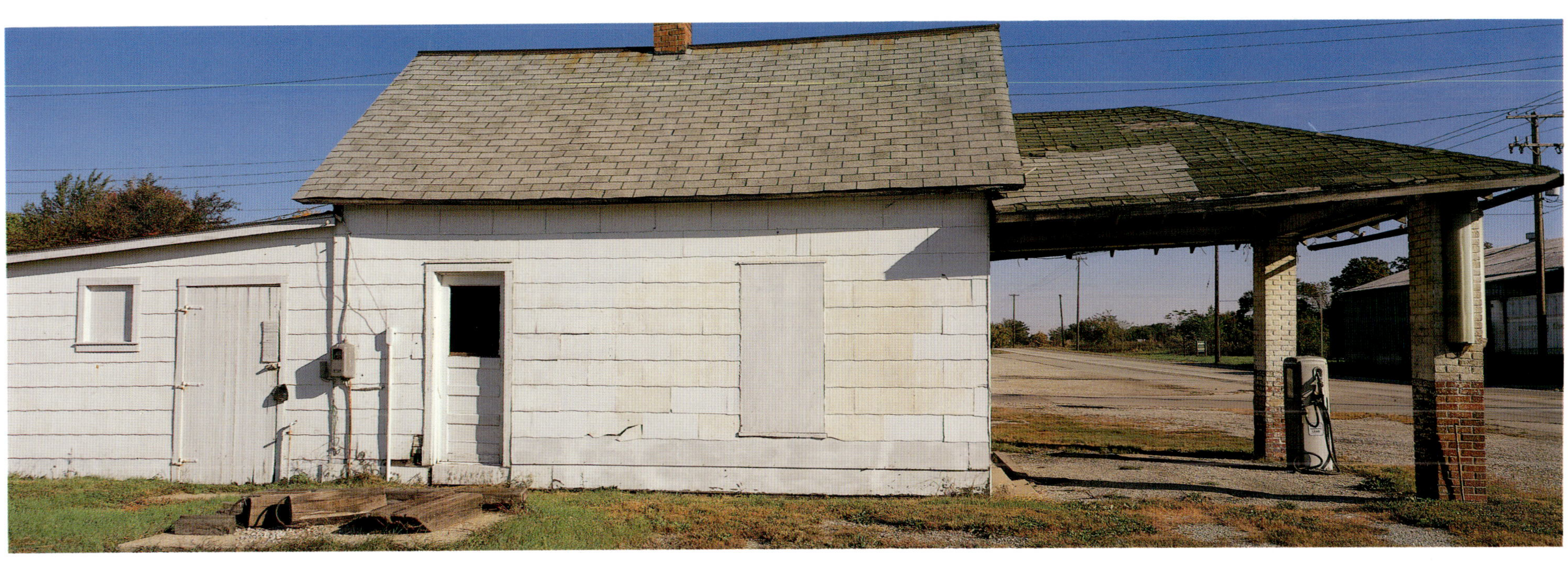

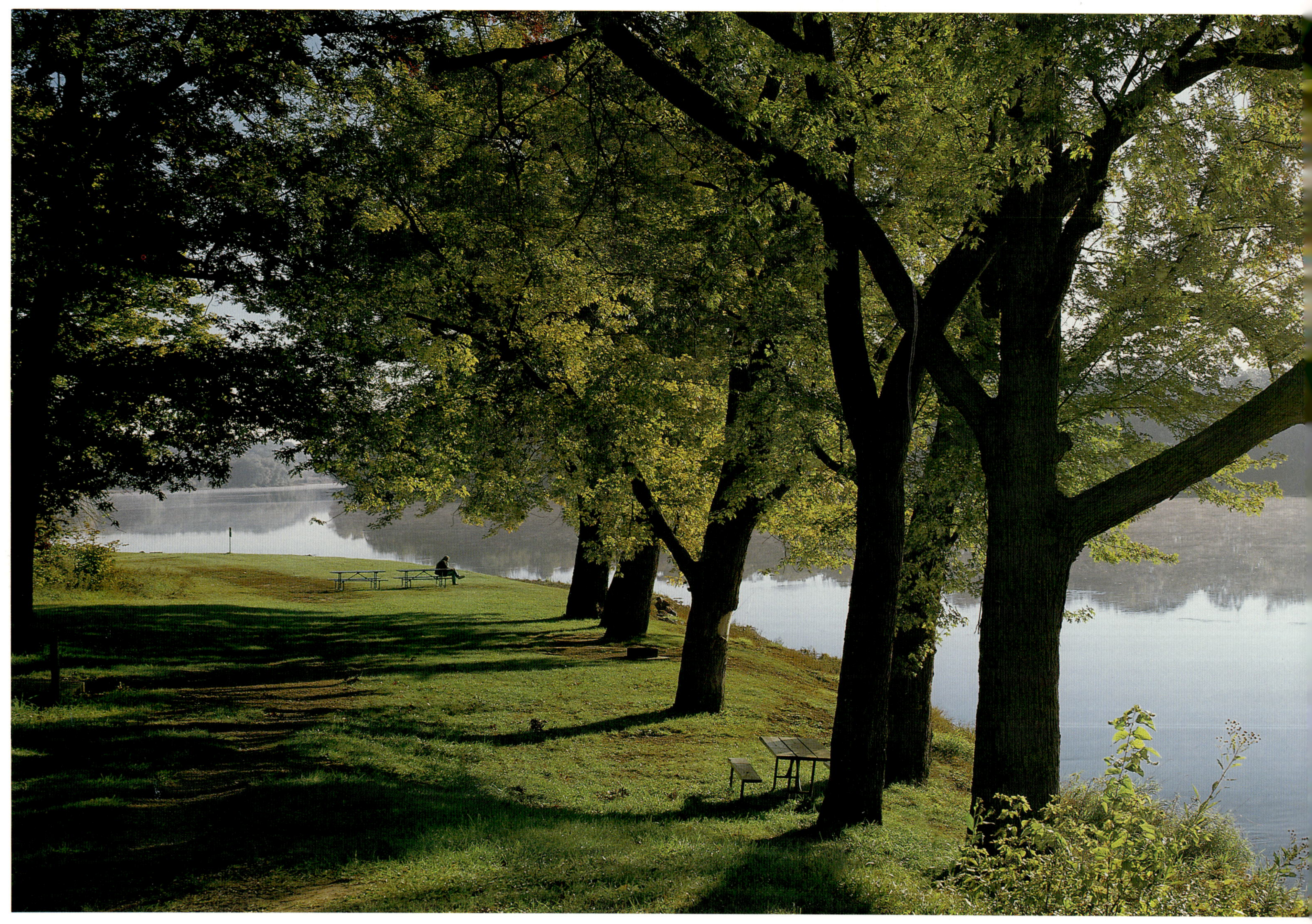

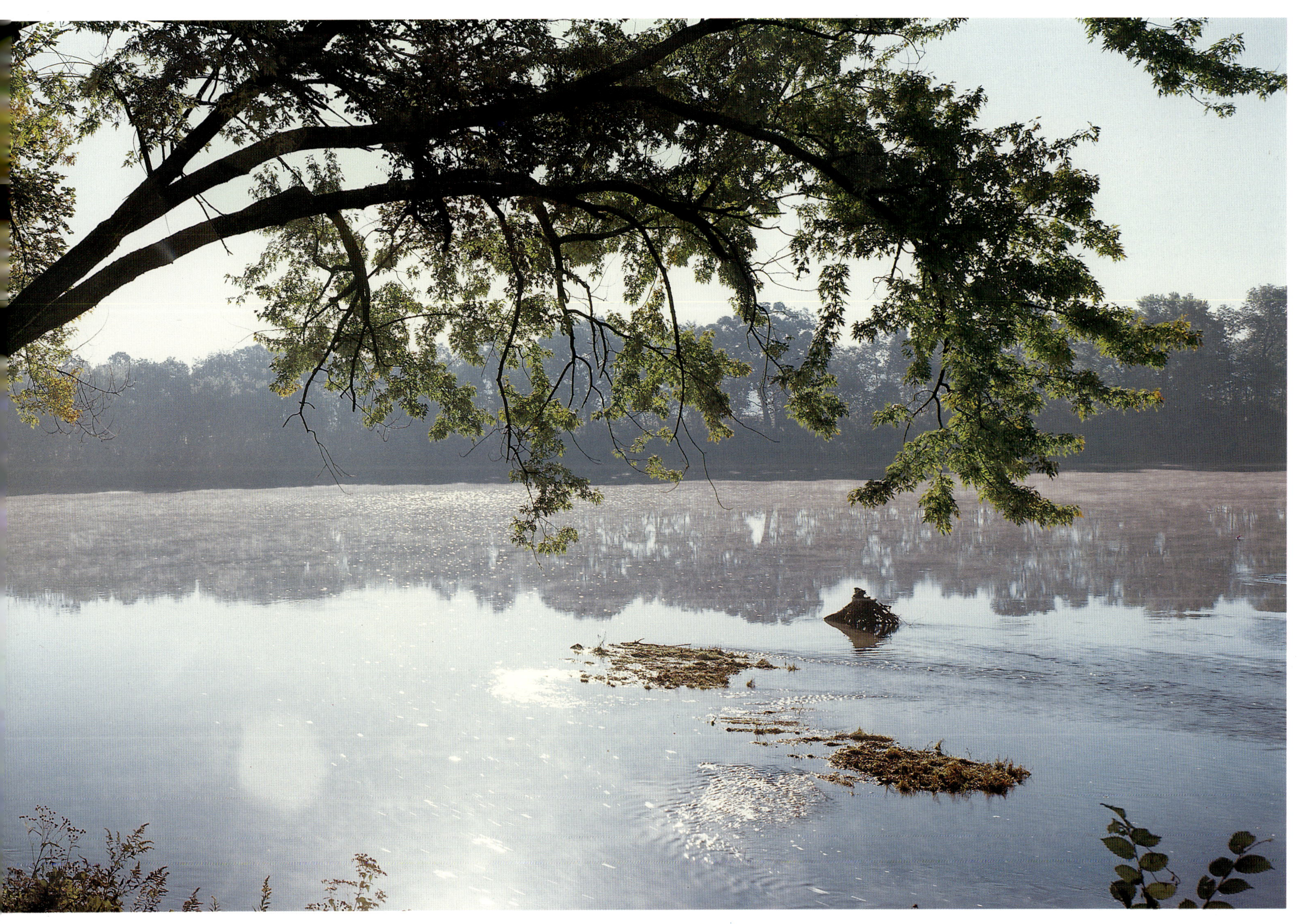

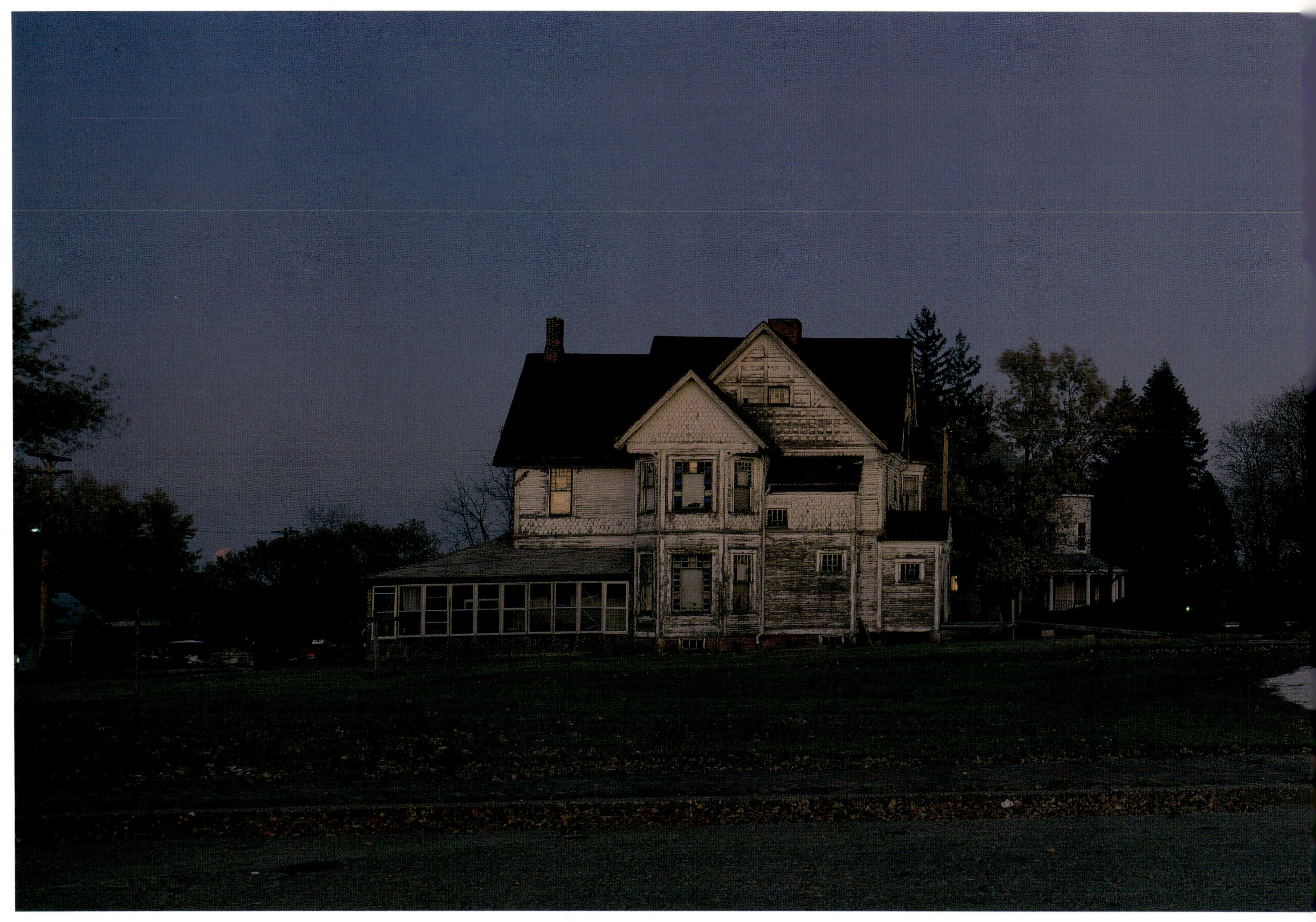

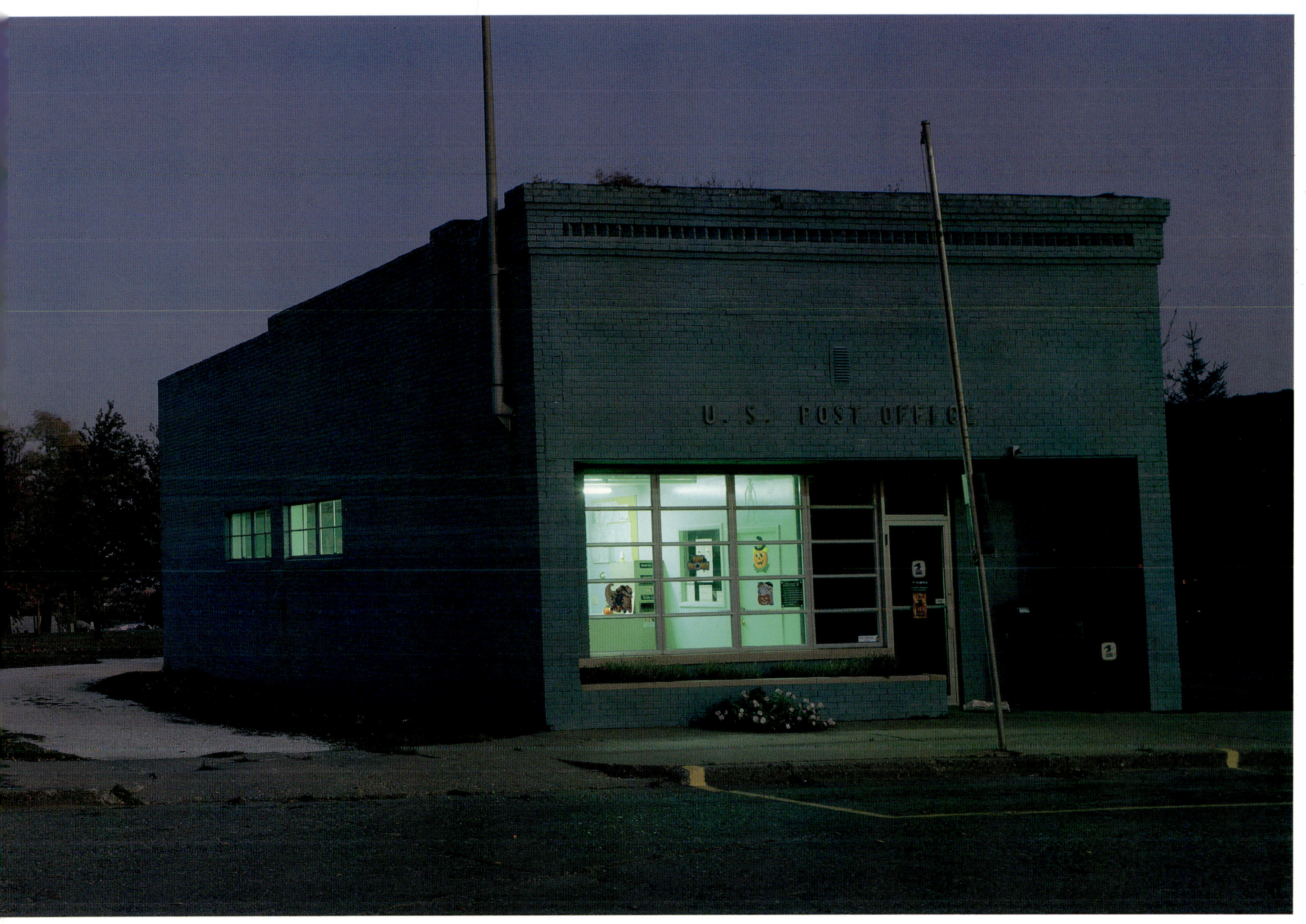
U. S. POST OFFICE

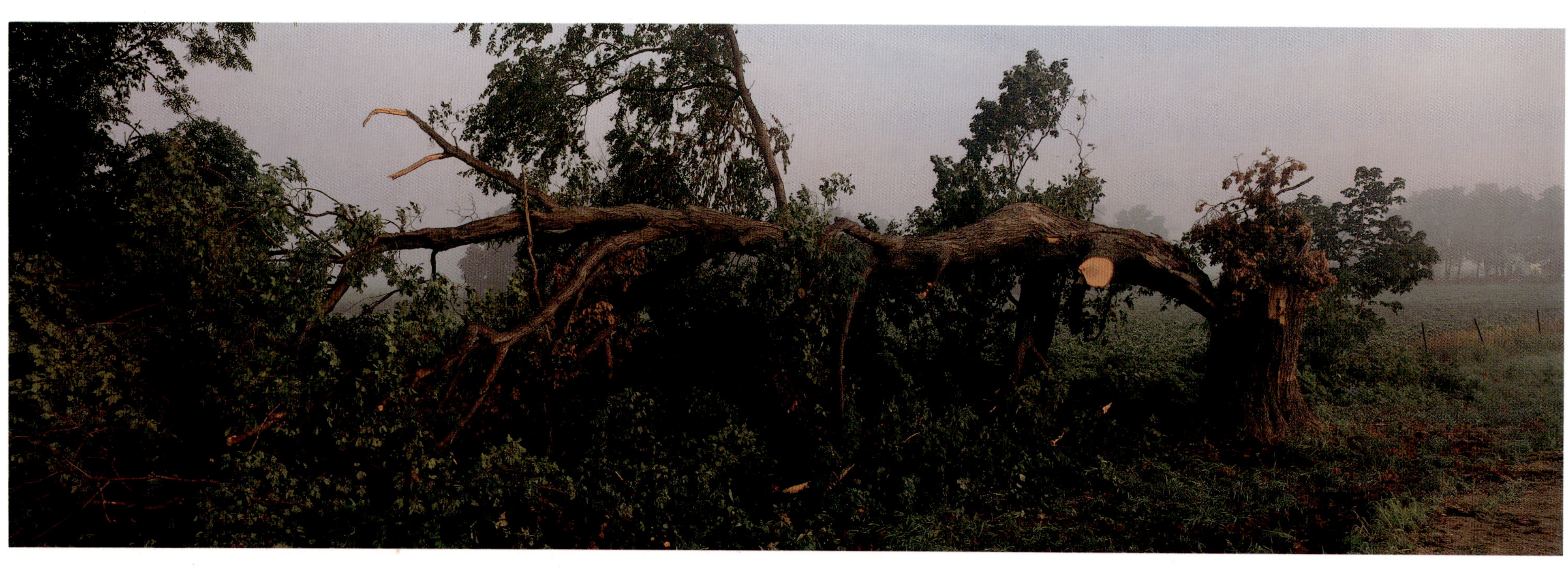

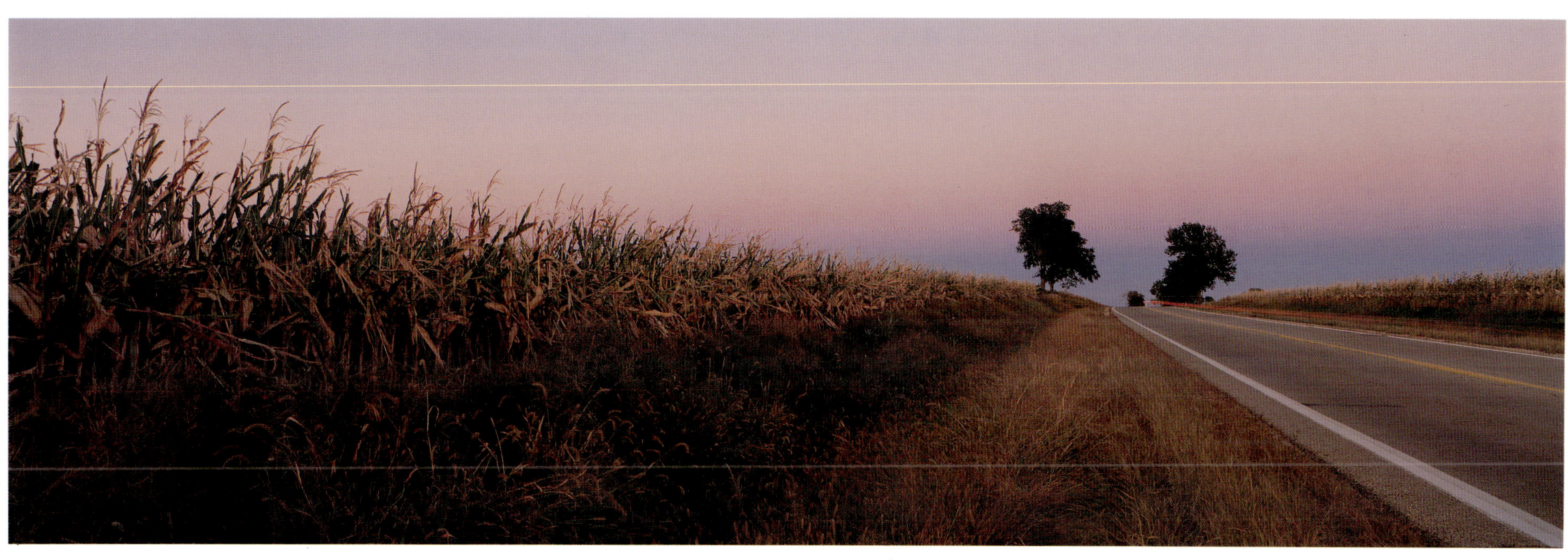

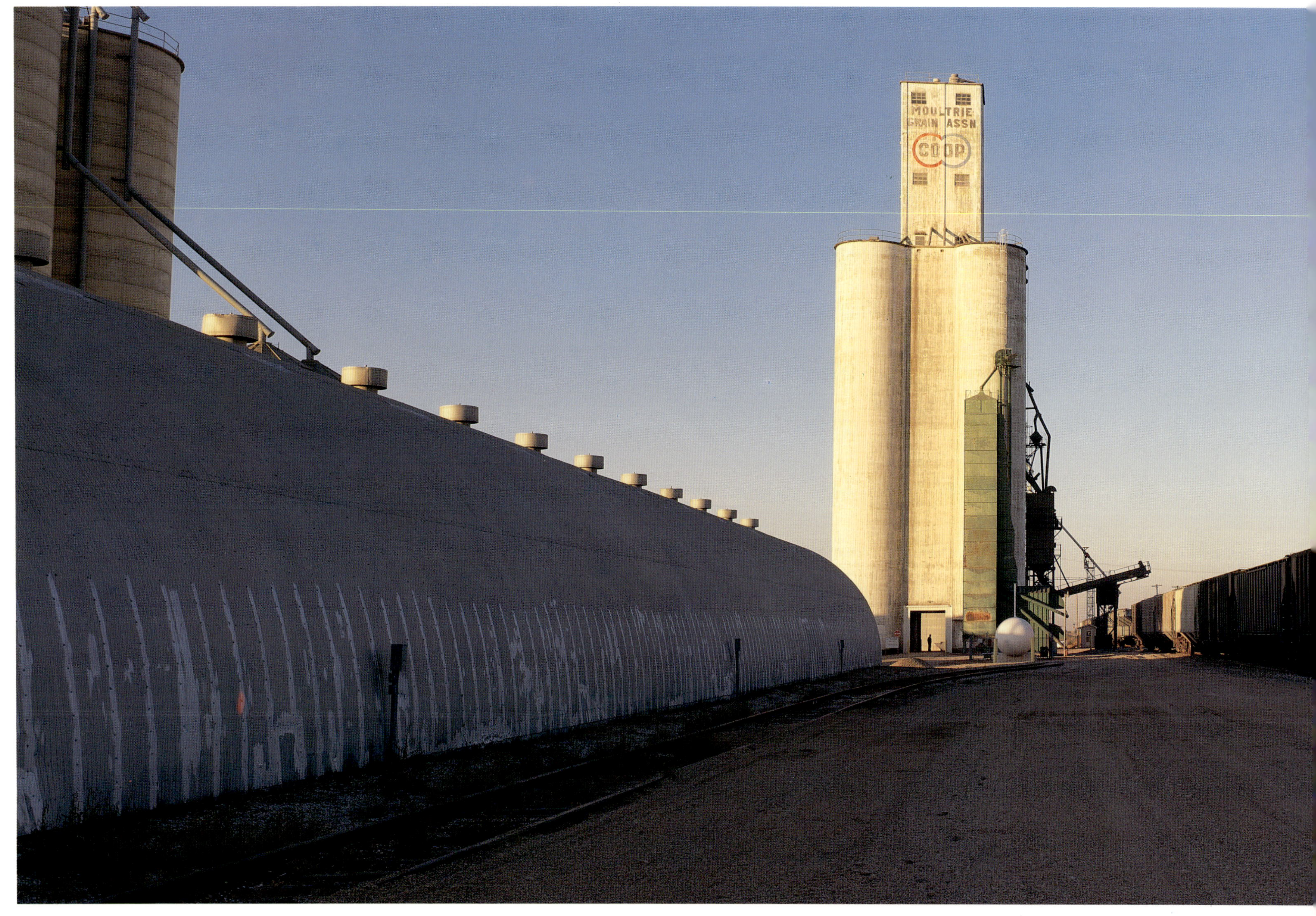
MOULTRIE
GRAIN ASSN
COOP

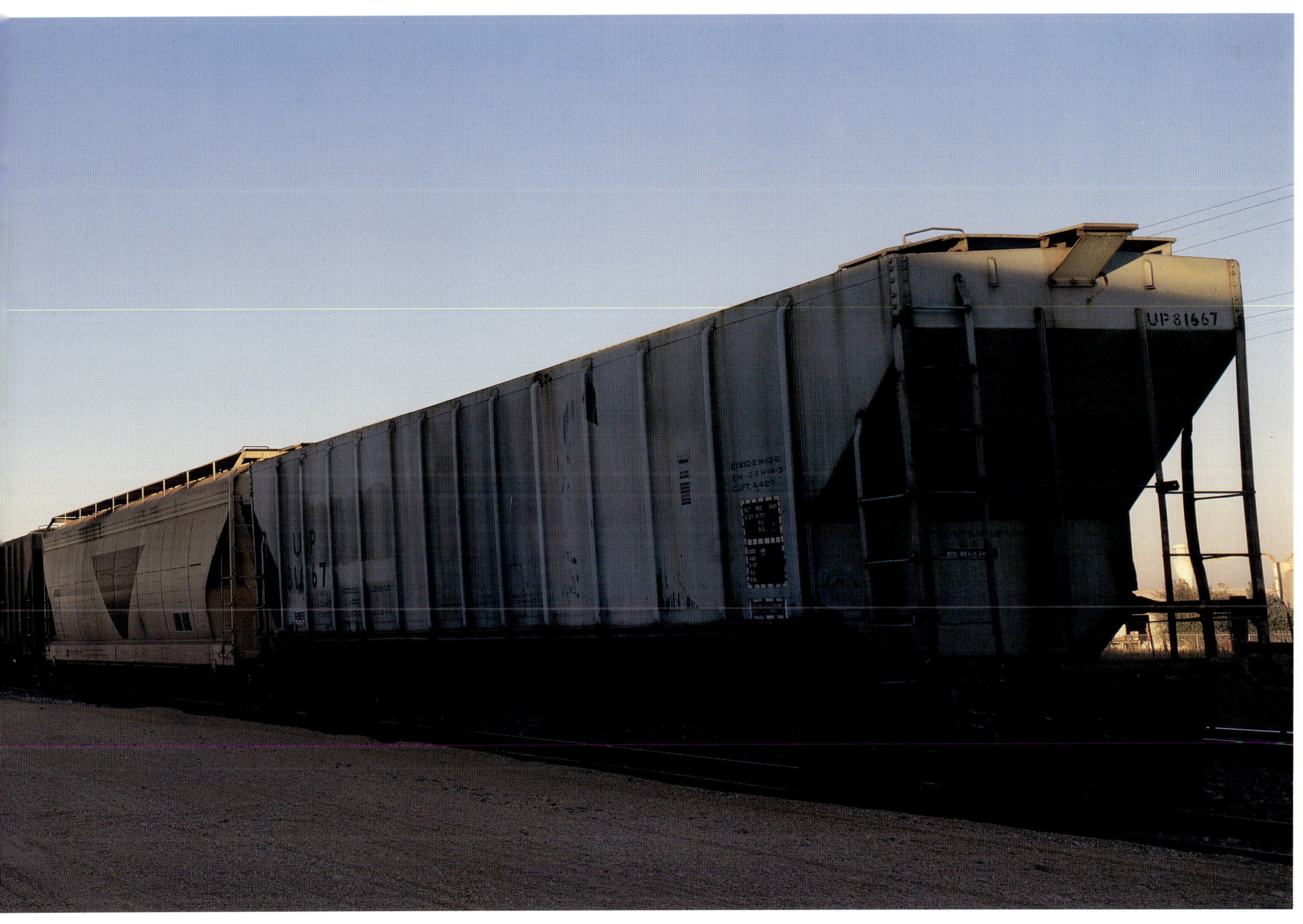
UP81667

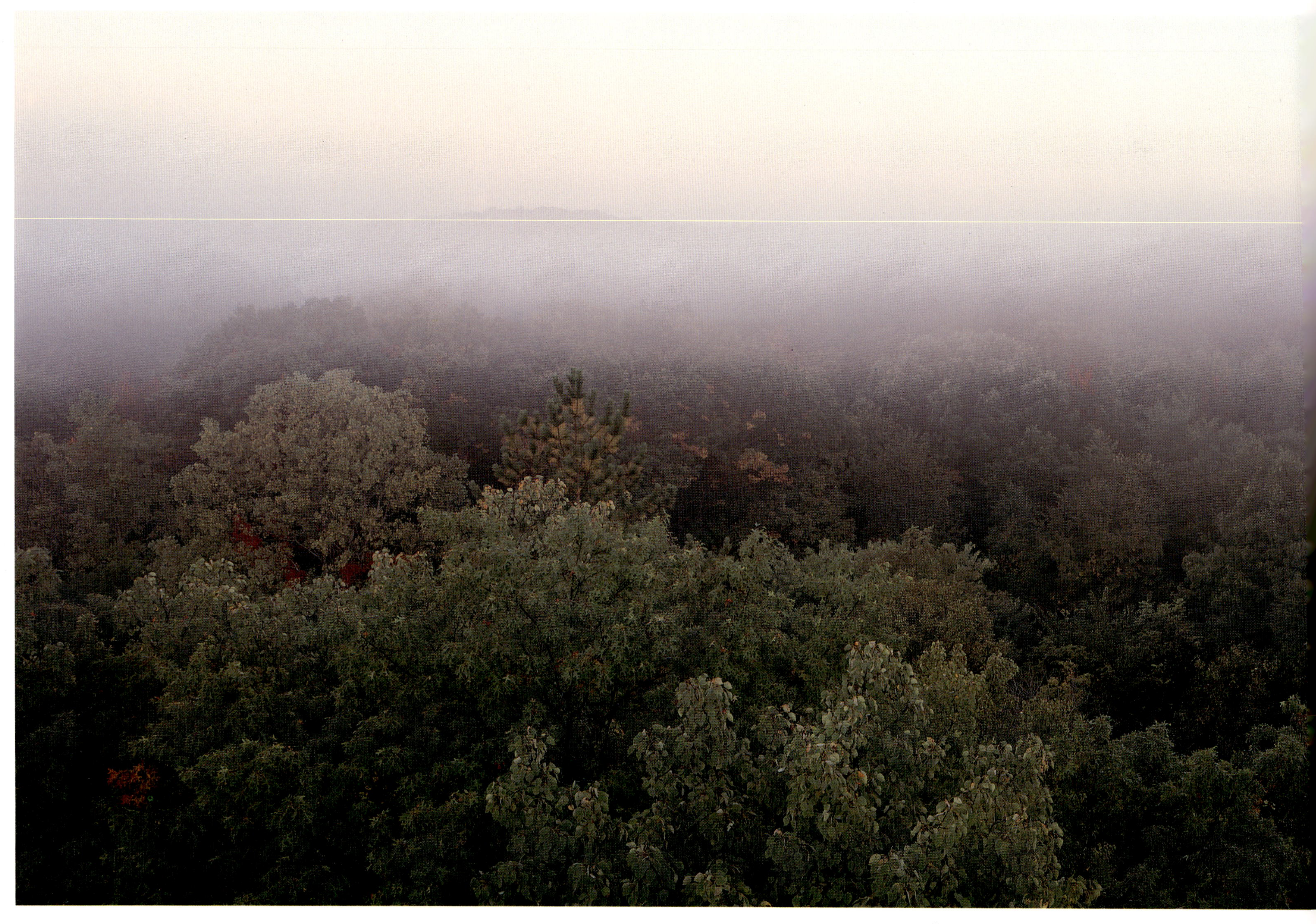

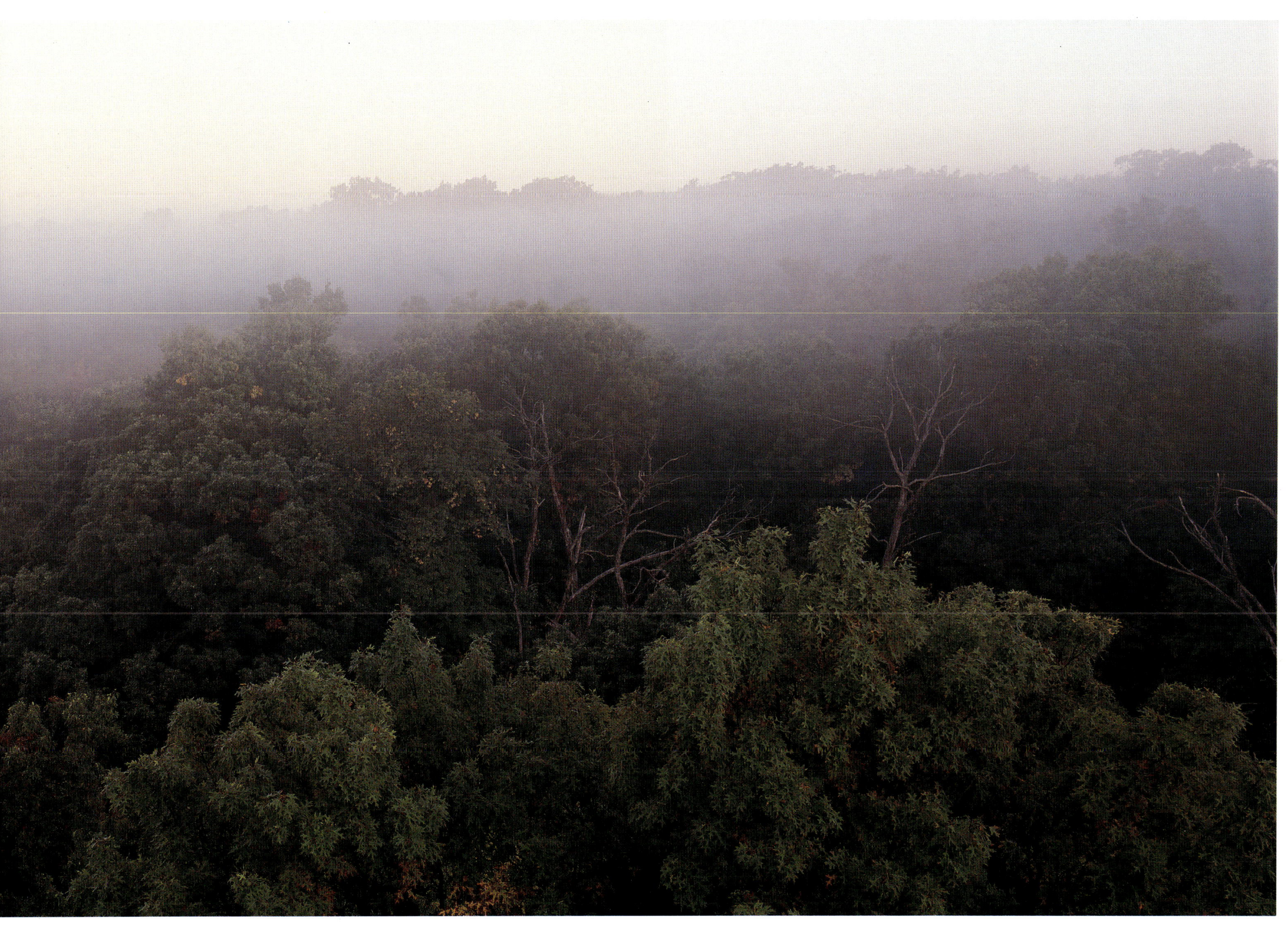

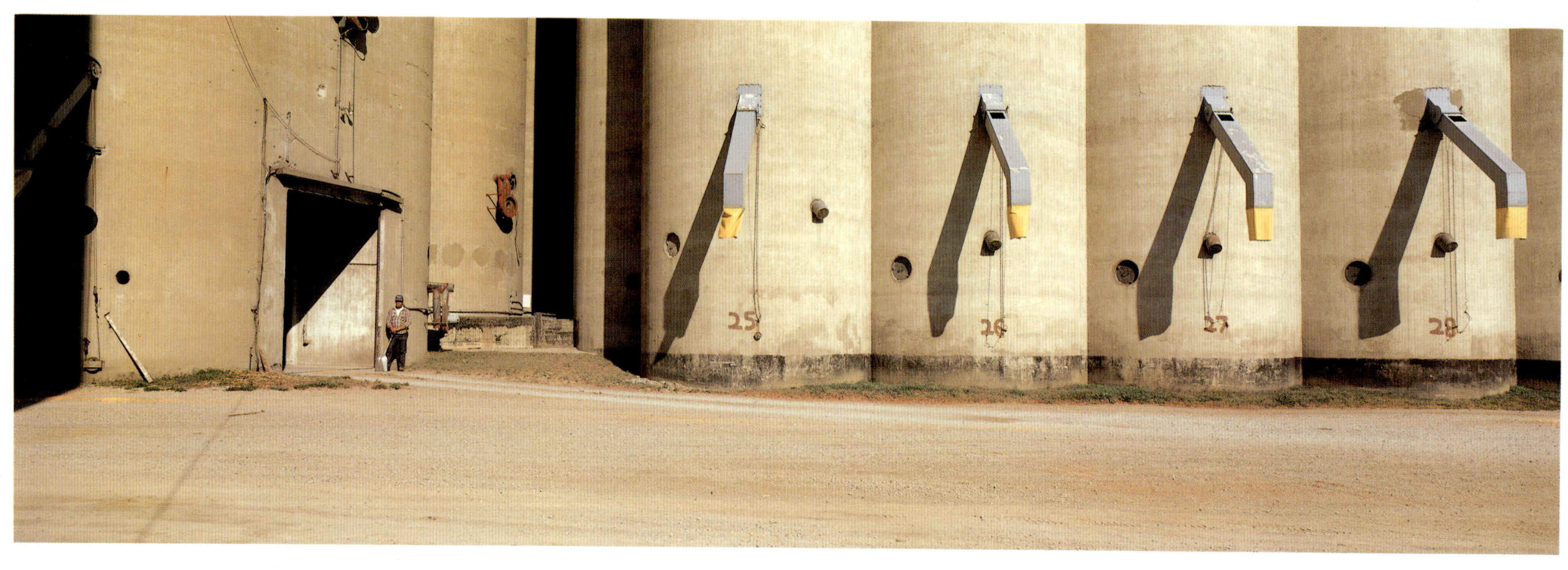
25
26
27
28

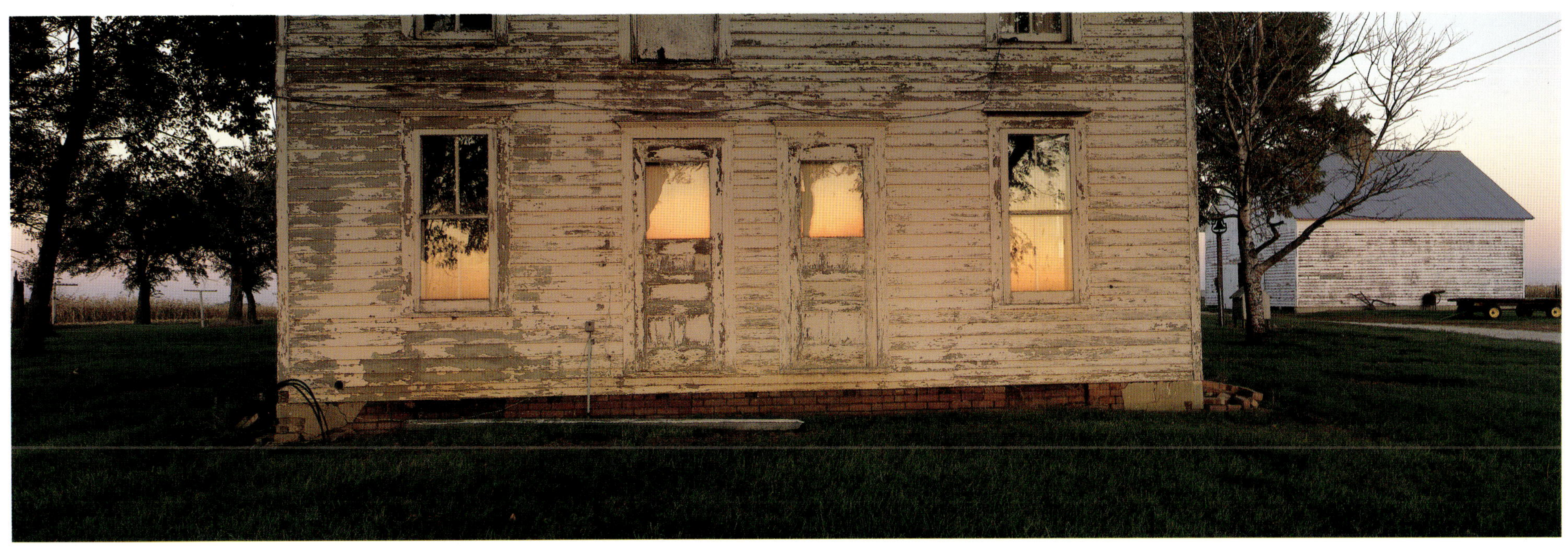

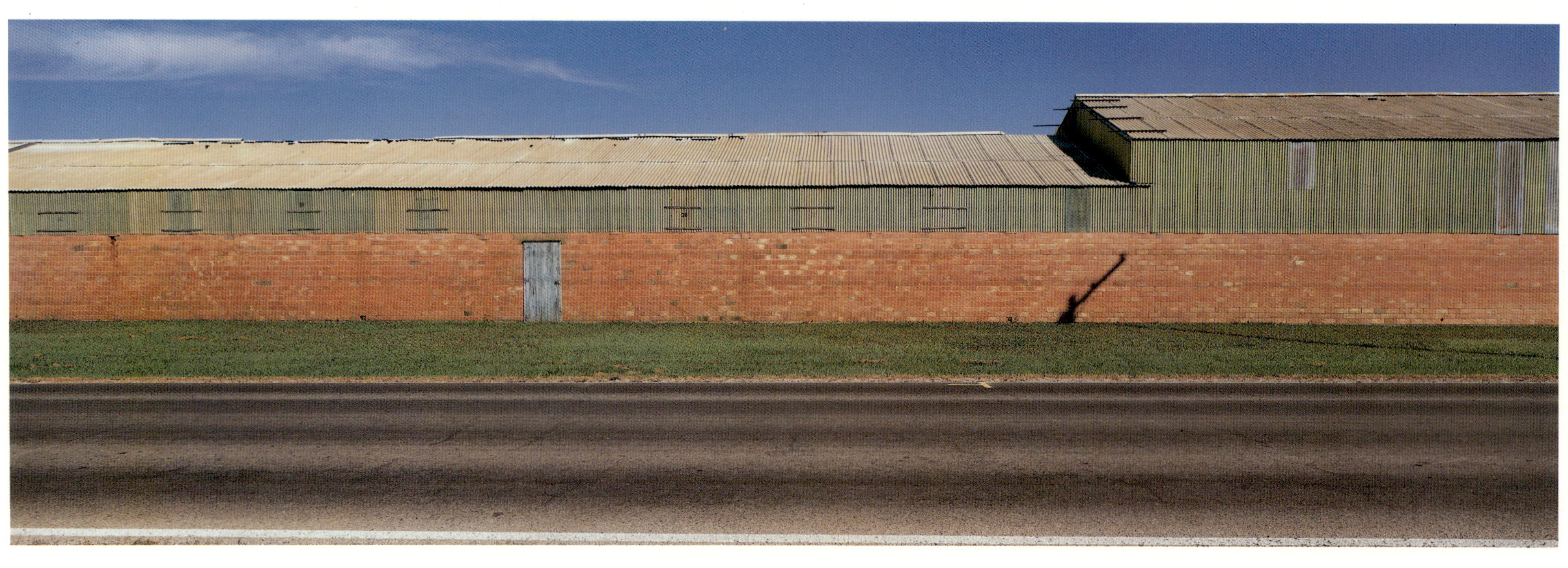

35

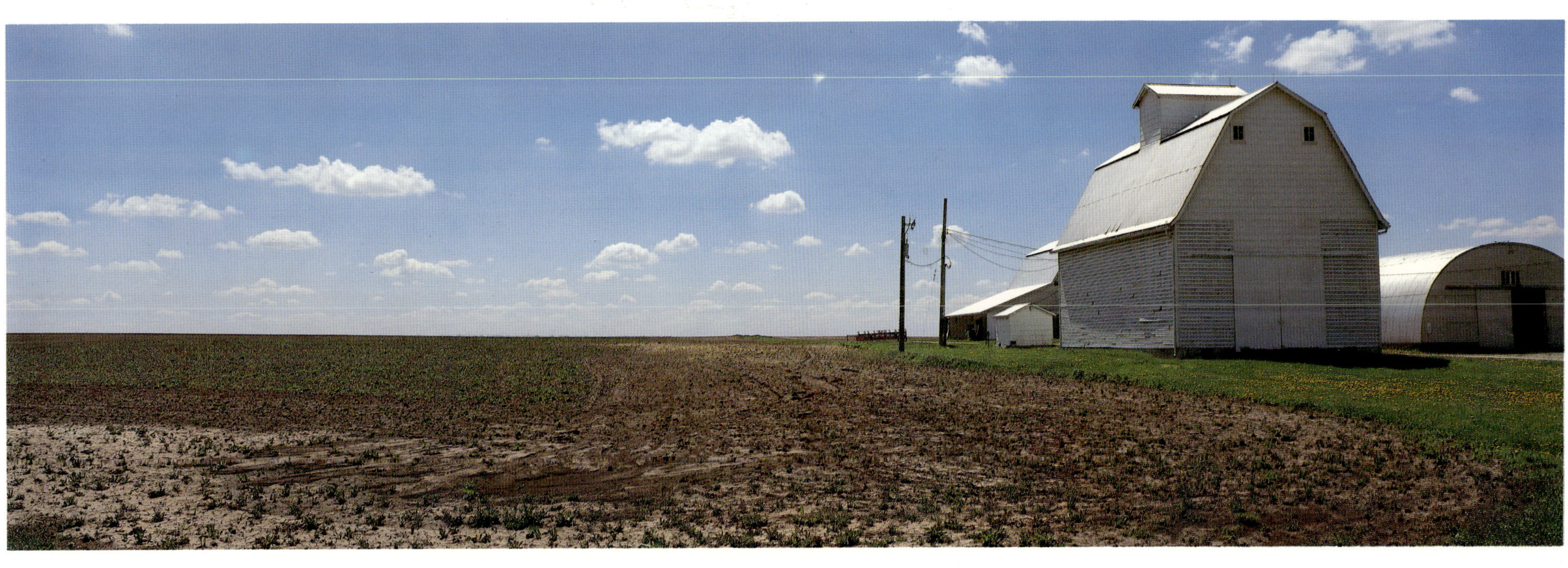

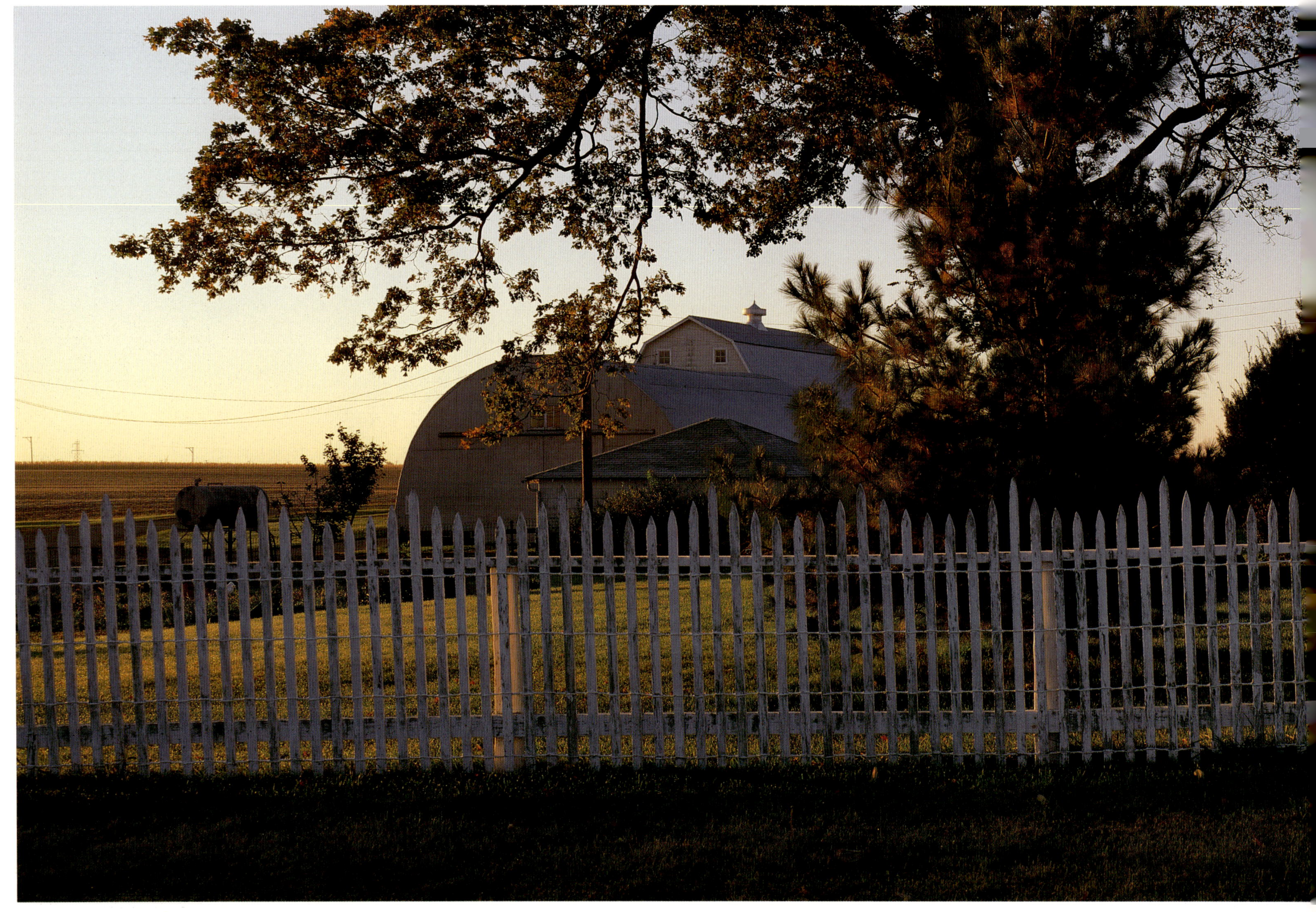

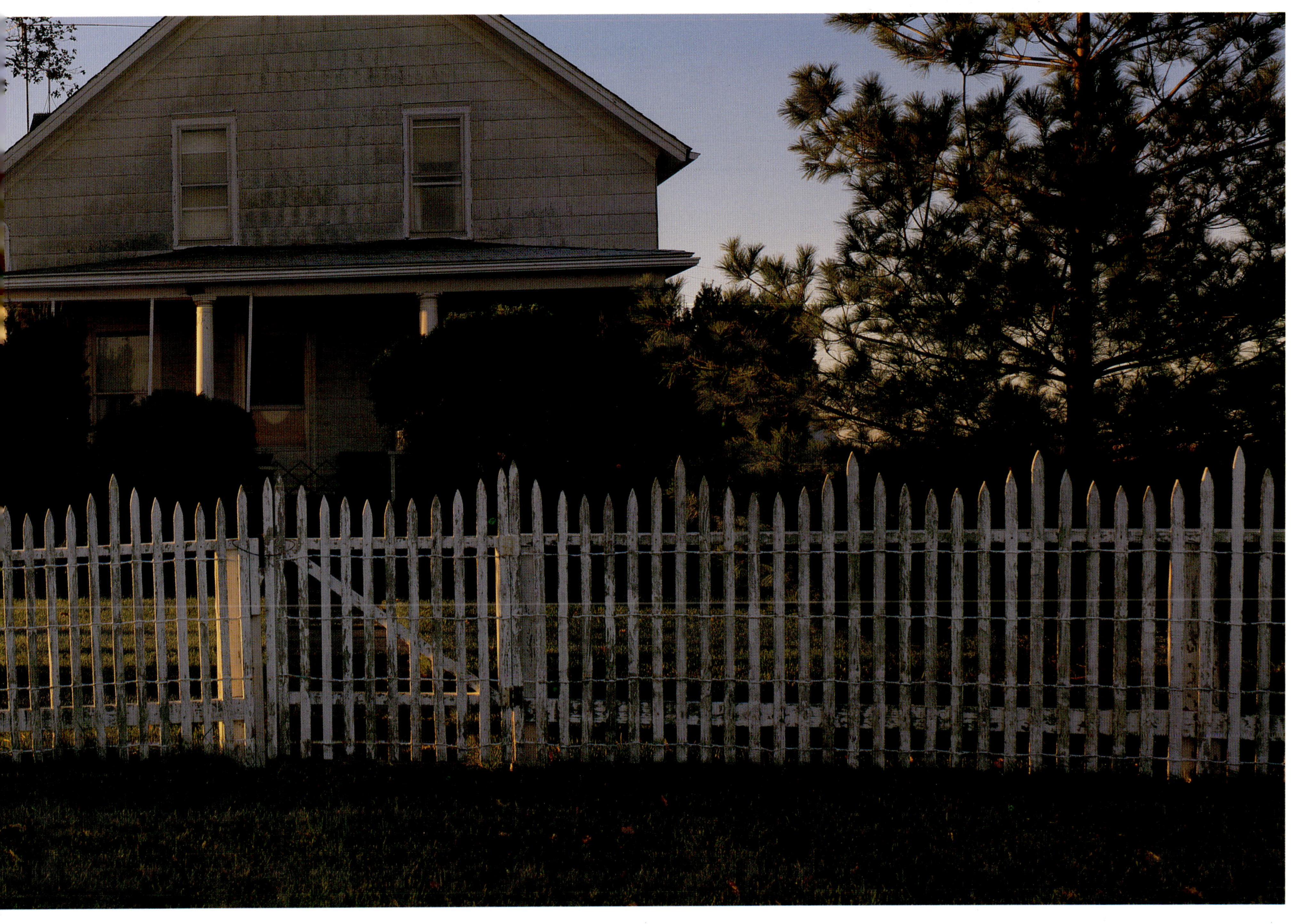

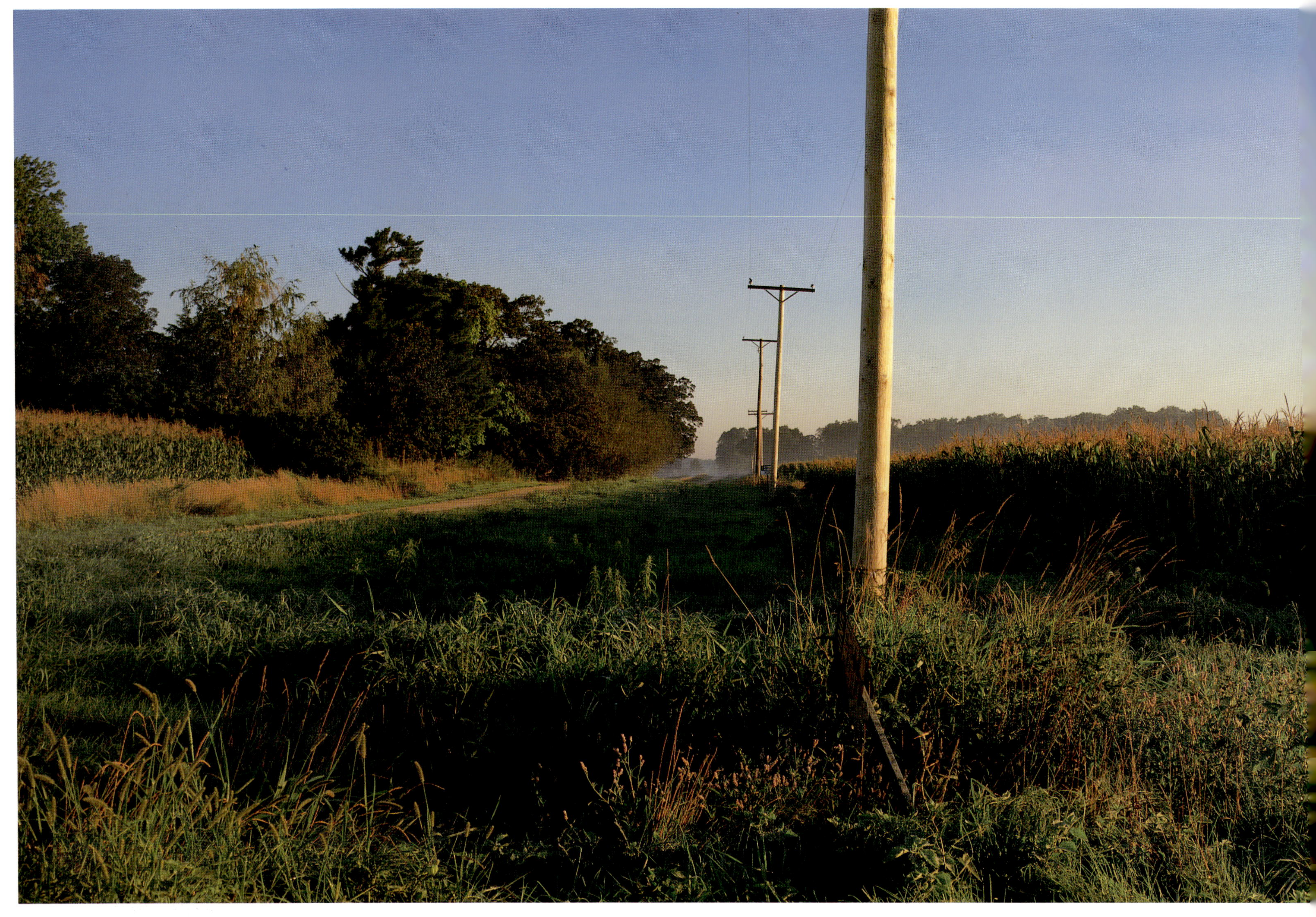

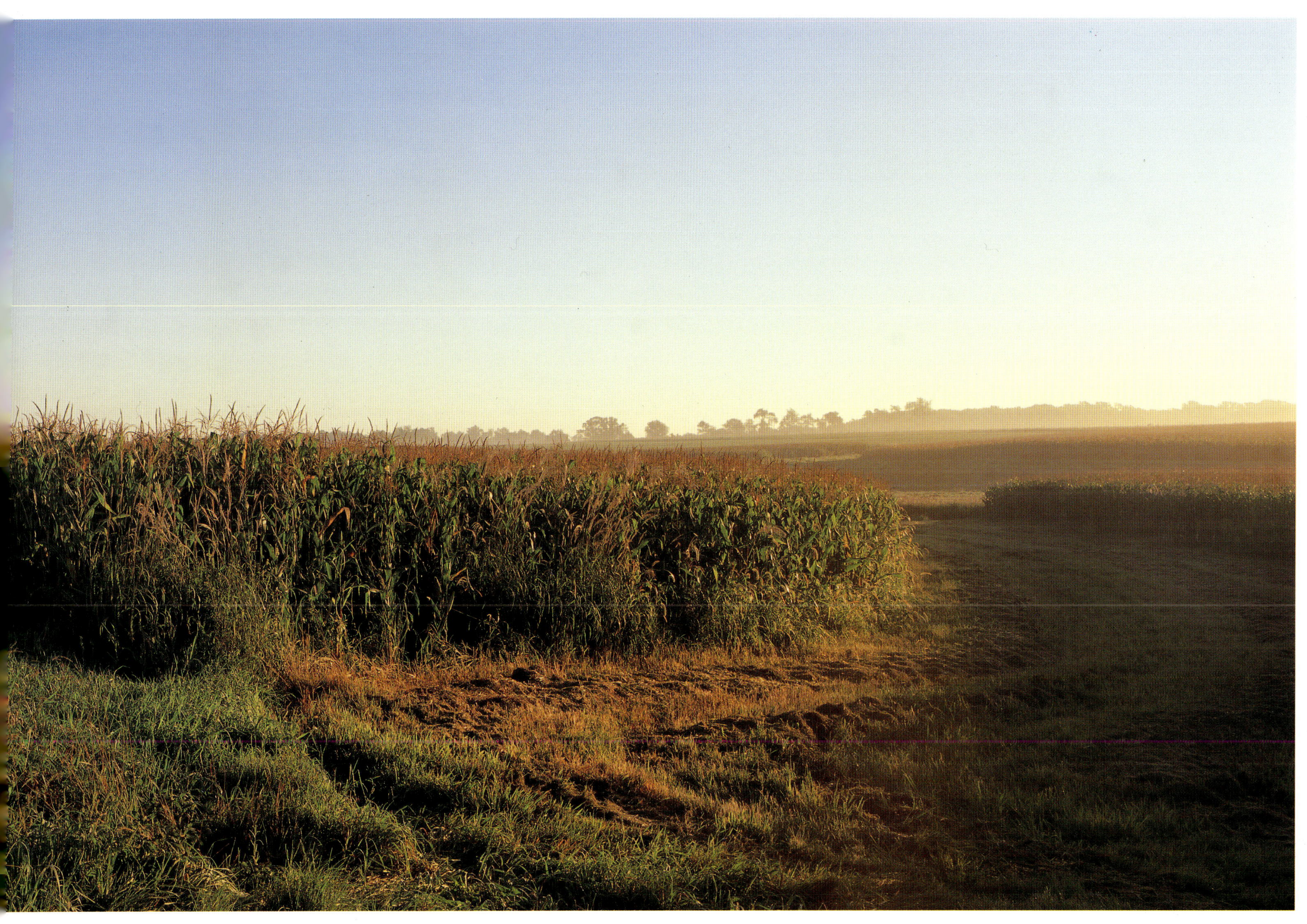

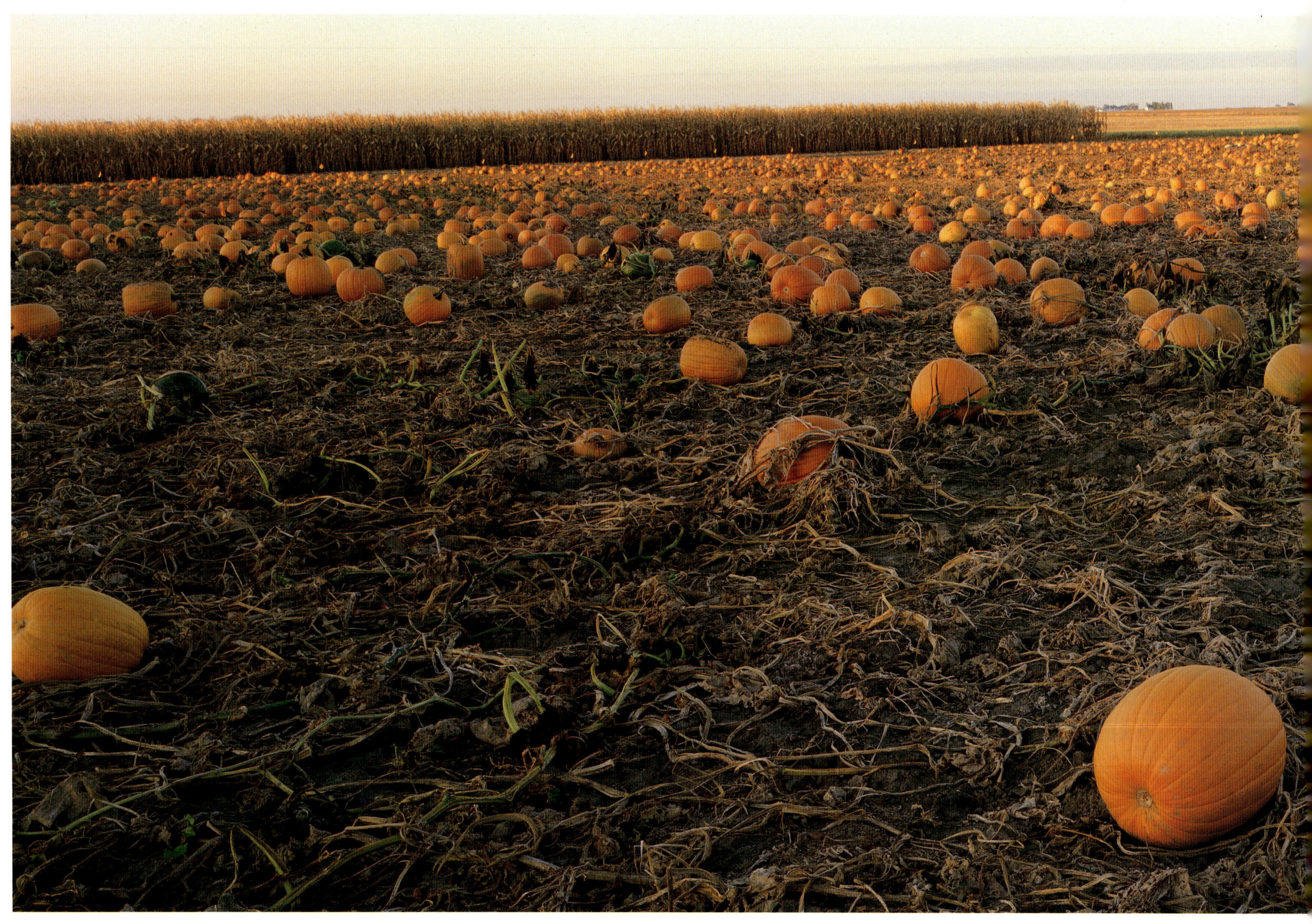

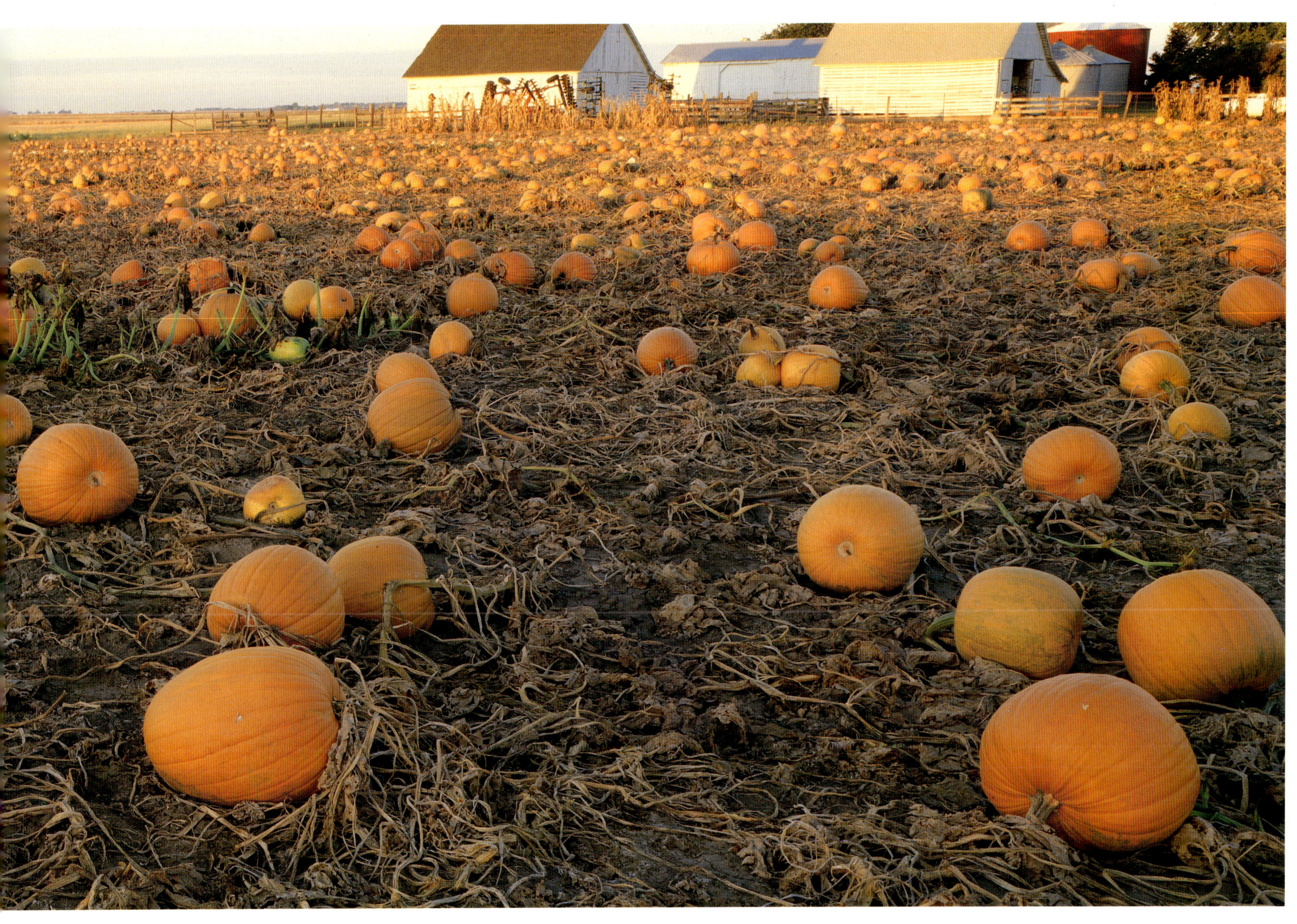

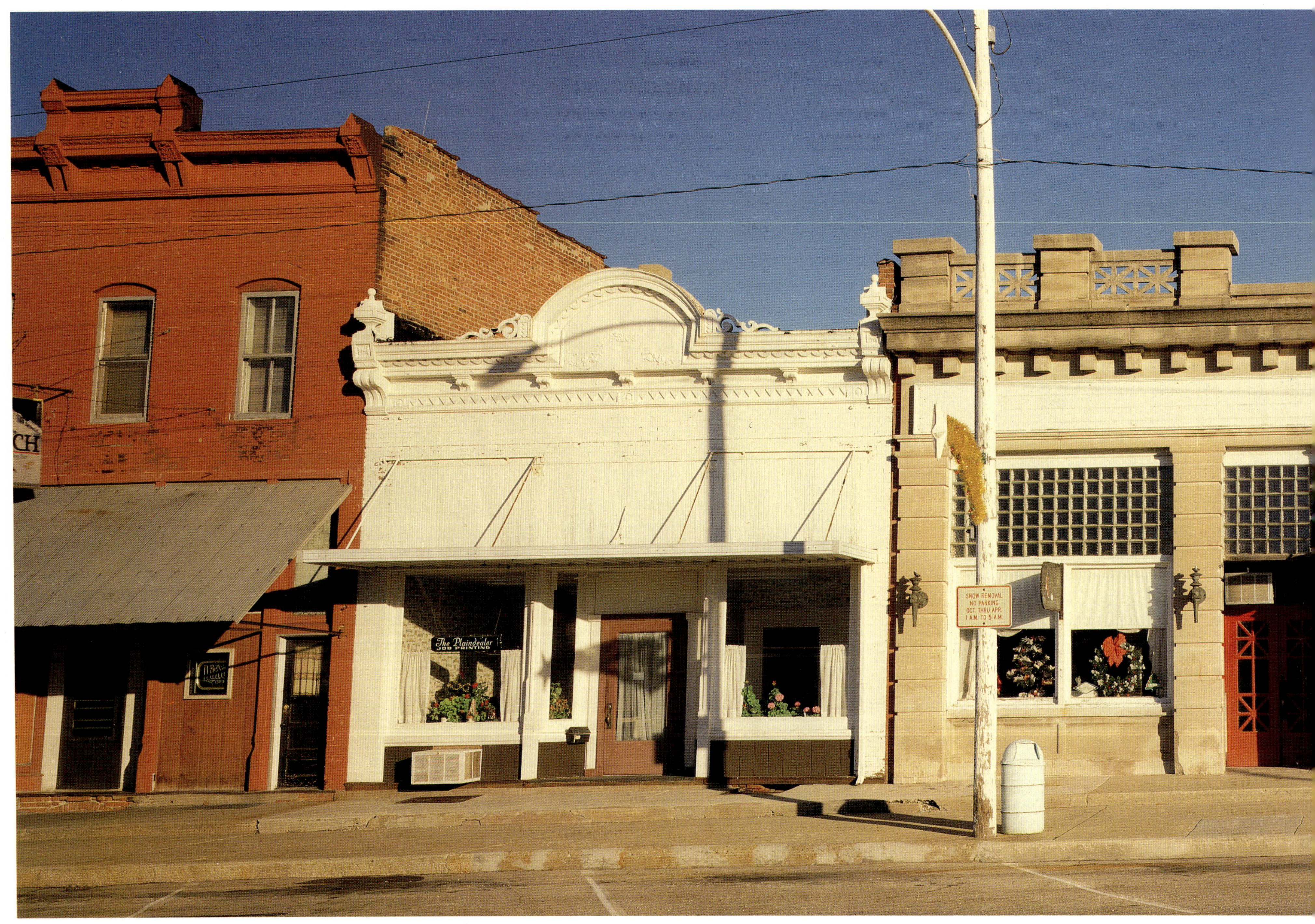
The Plaindealer
JOB PRINTING
SNOW REMOVAL
NO PARKING
OCT. THRU APR.
1 A.M. TO 5 A.M.

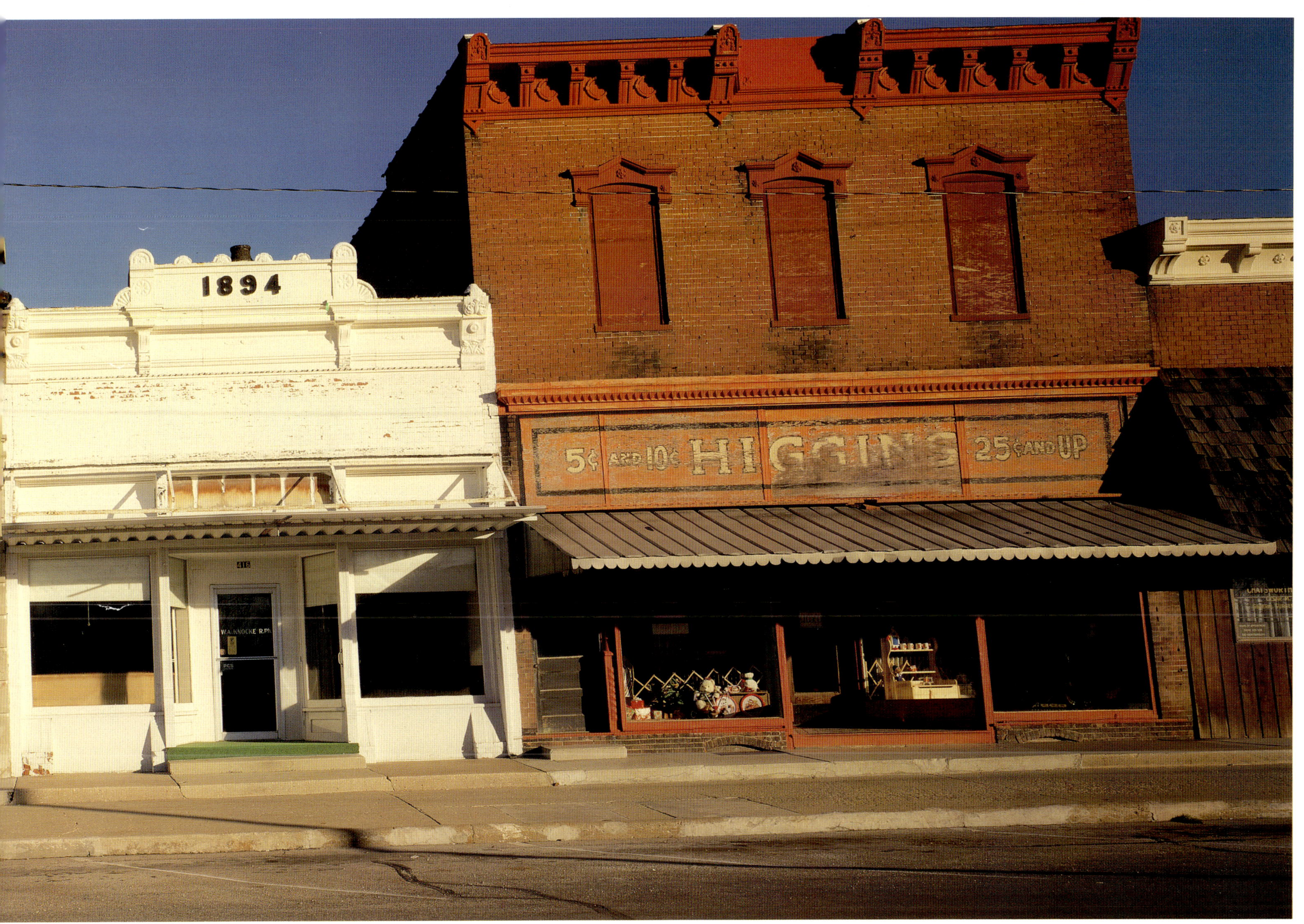
1894
5¢ AND 10¢
HIGGINS
25¢ AND UP

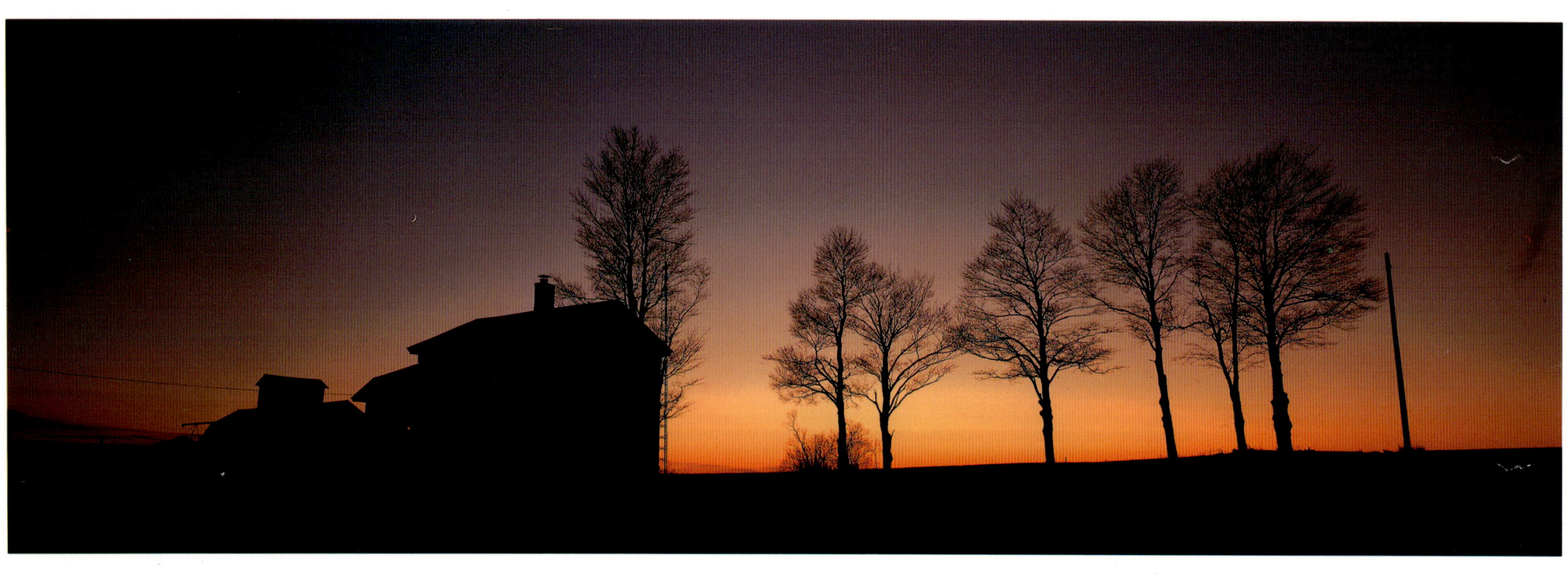

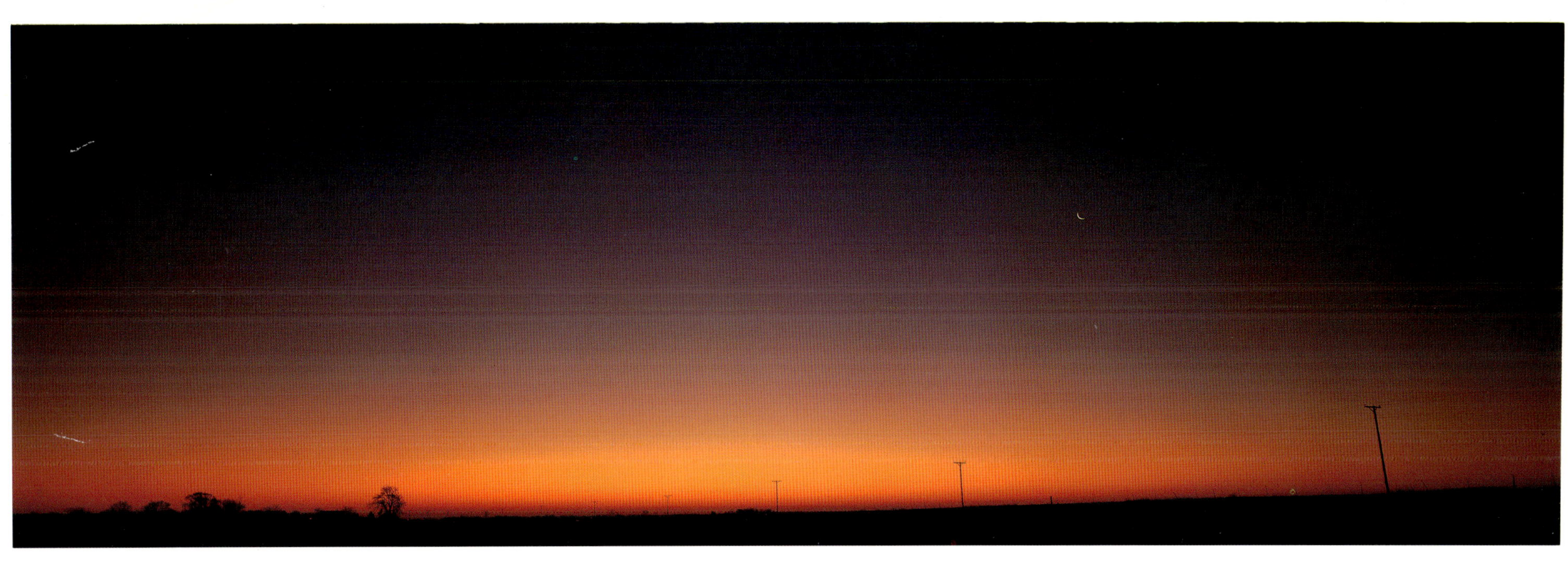

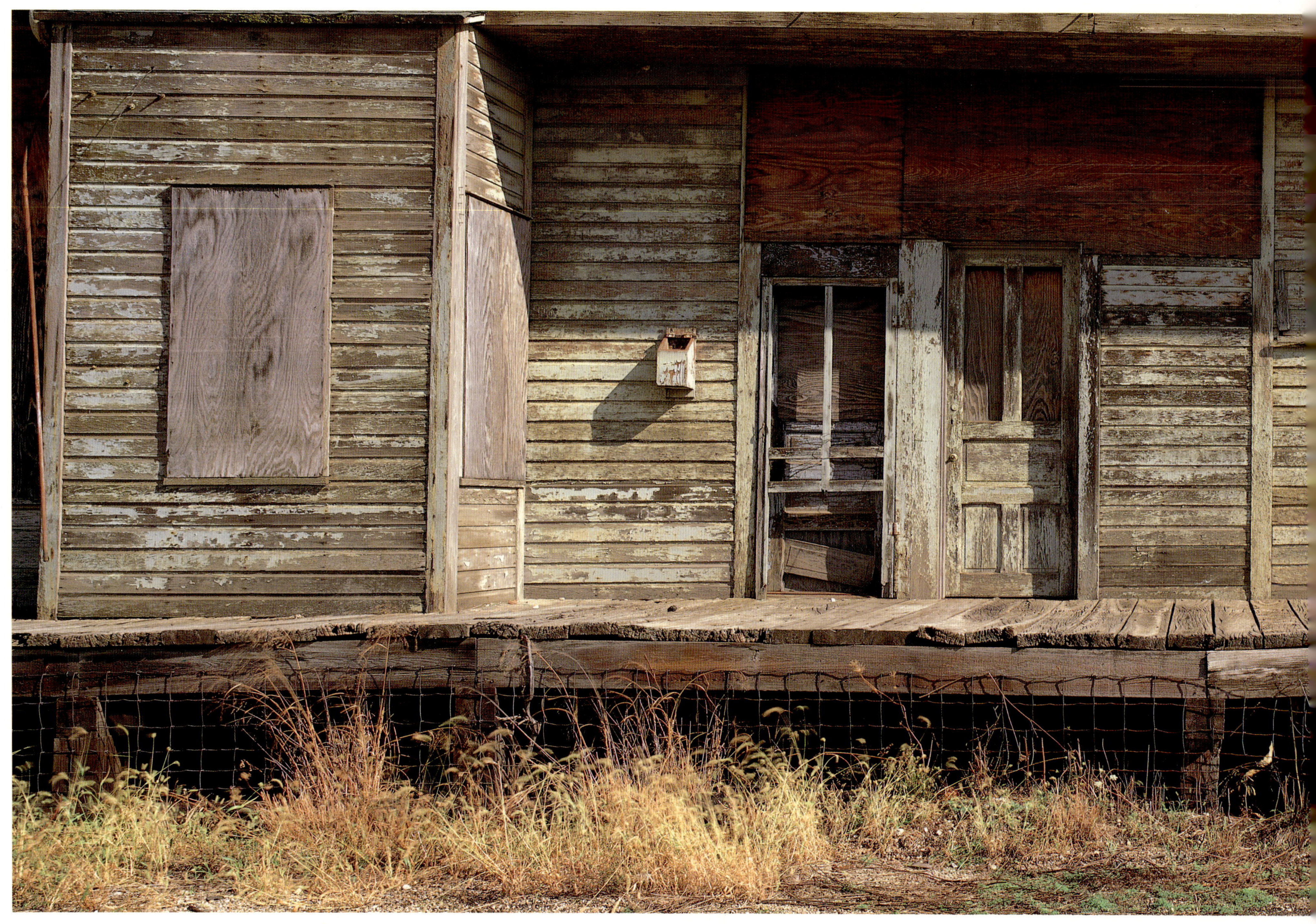

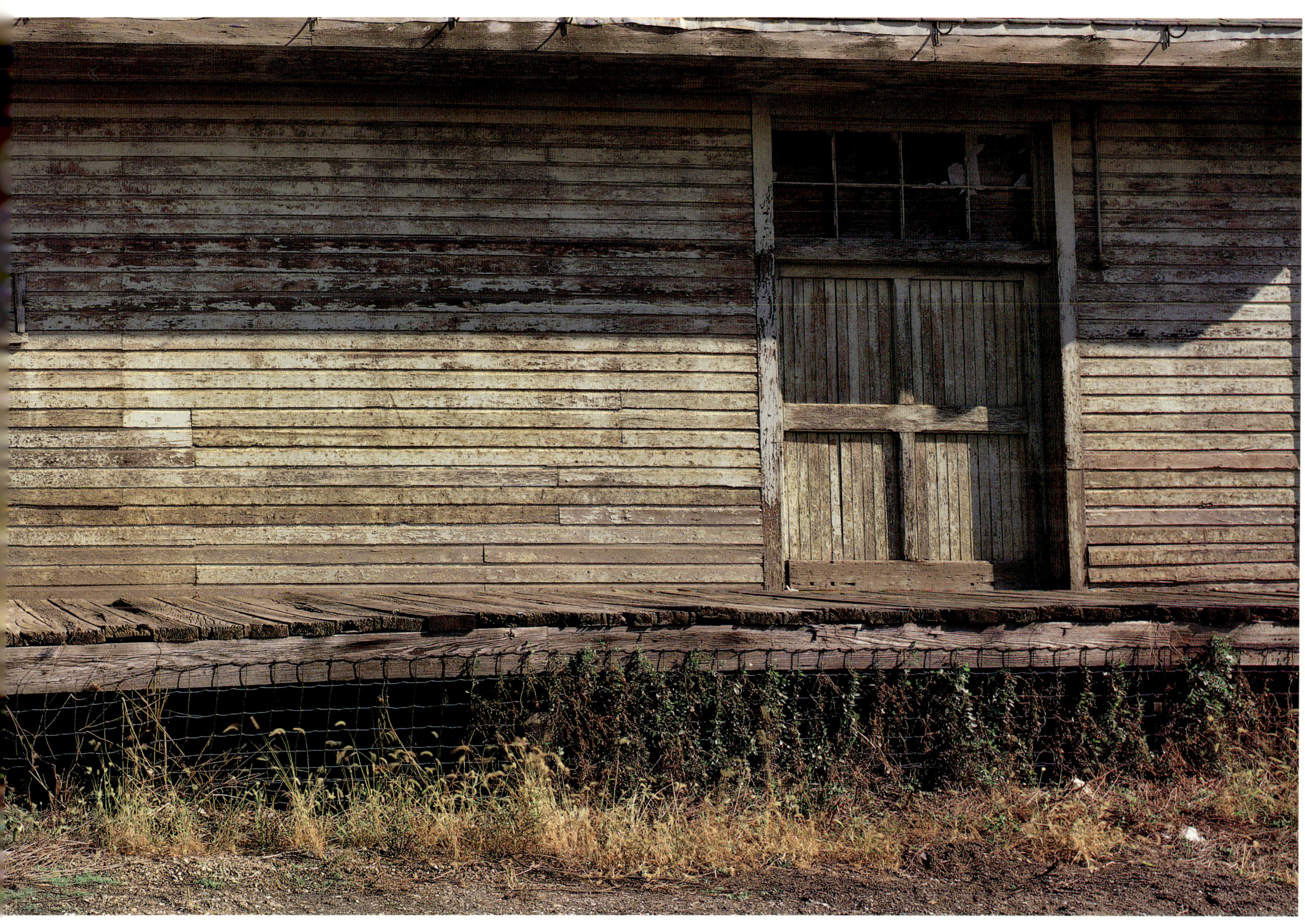

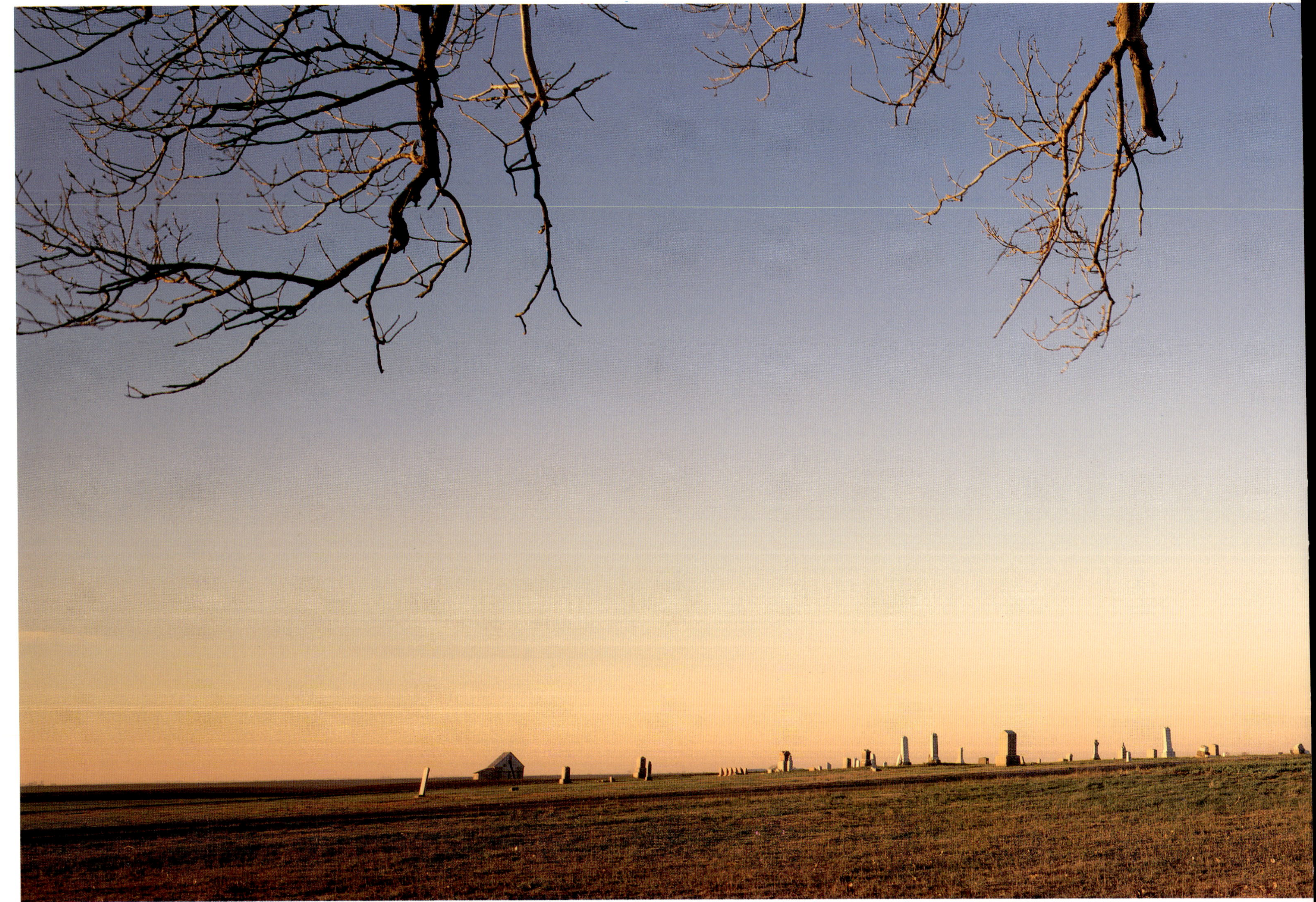

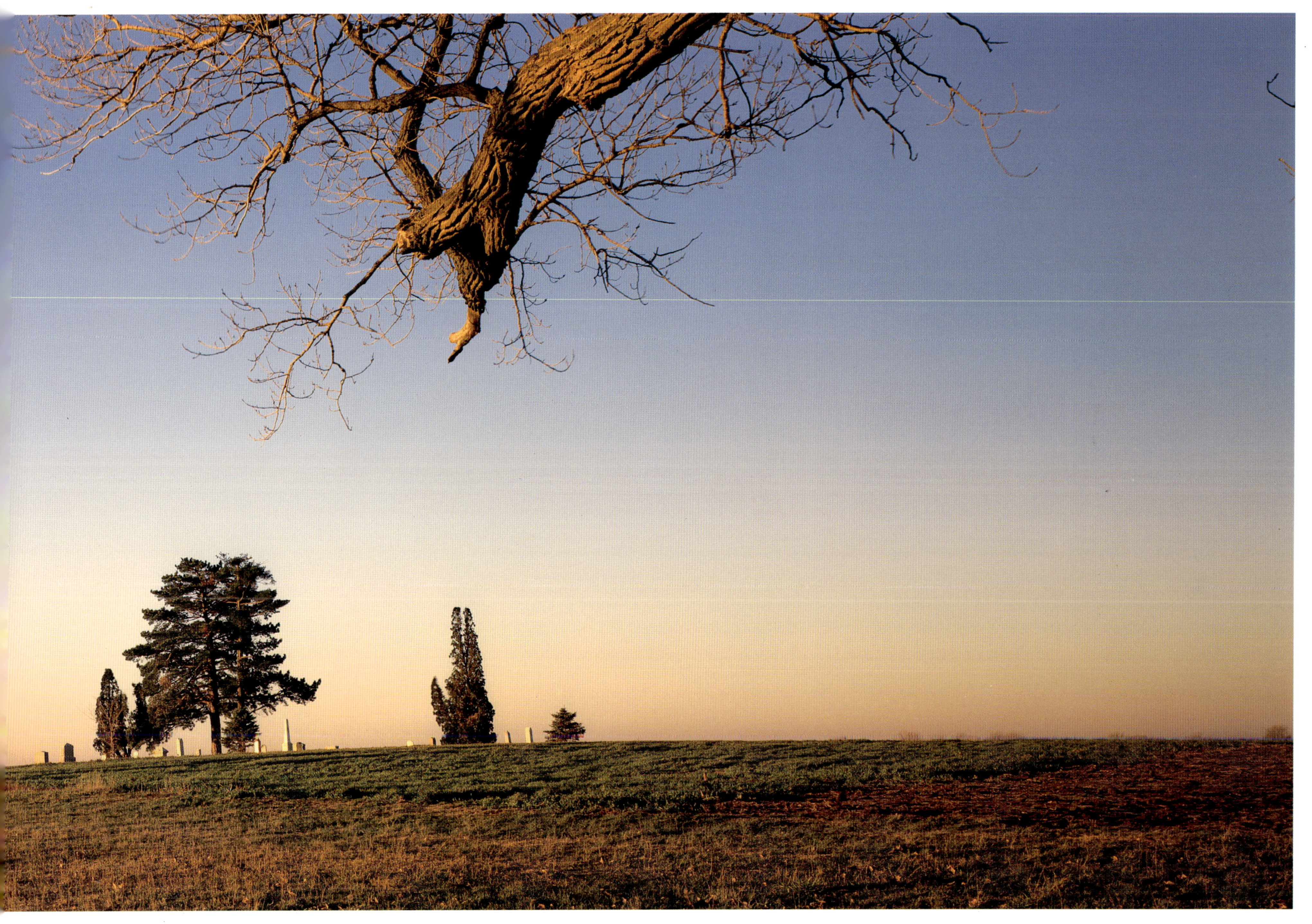

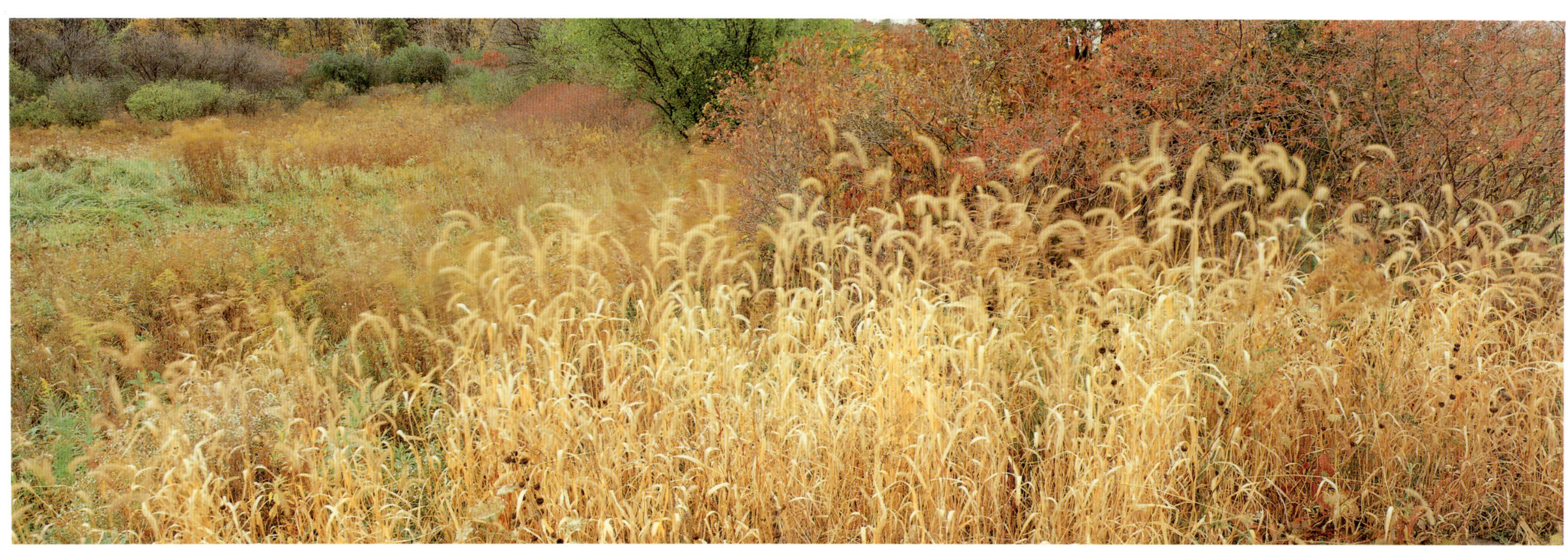

45

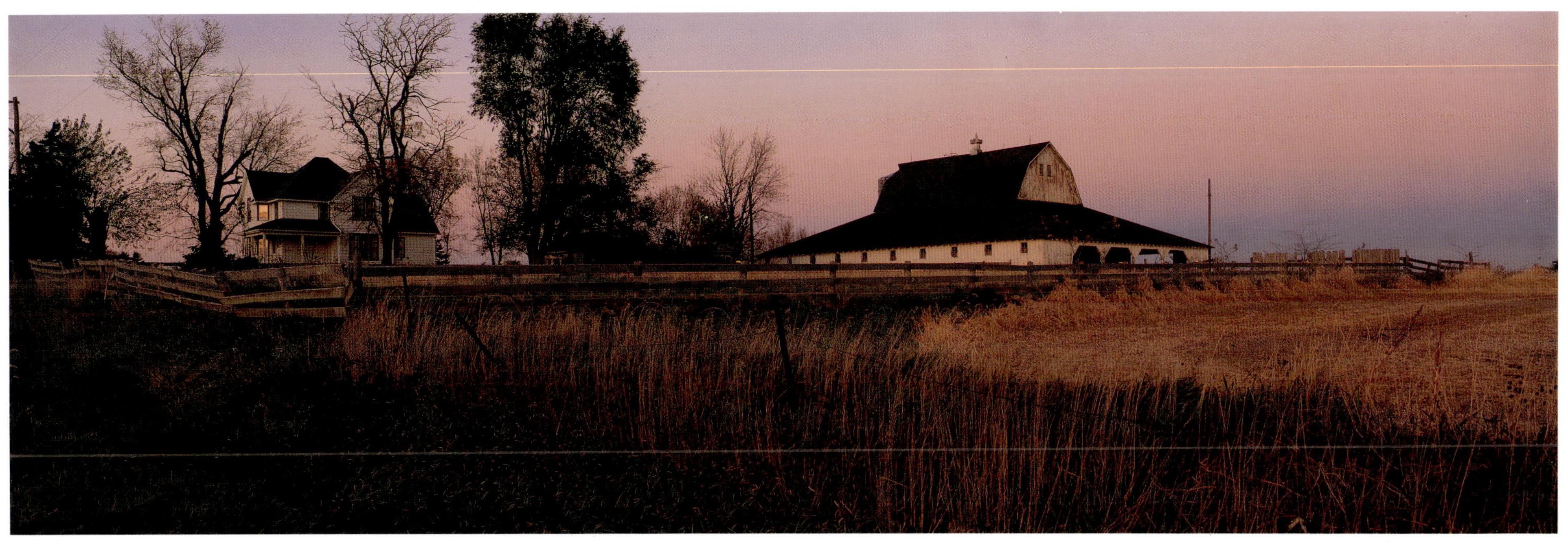

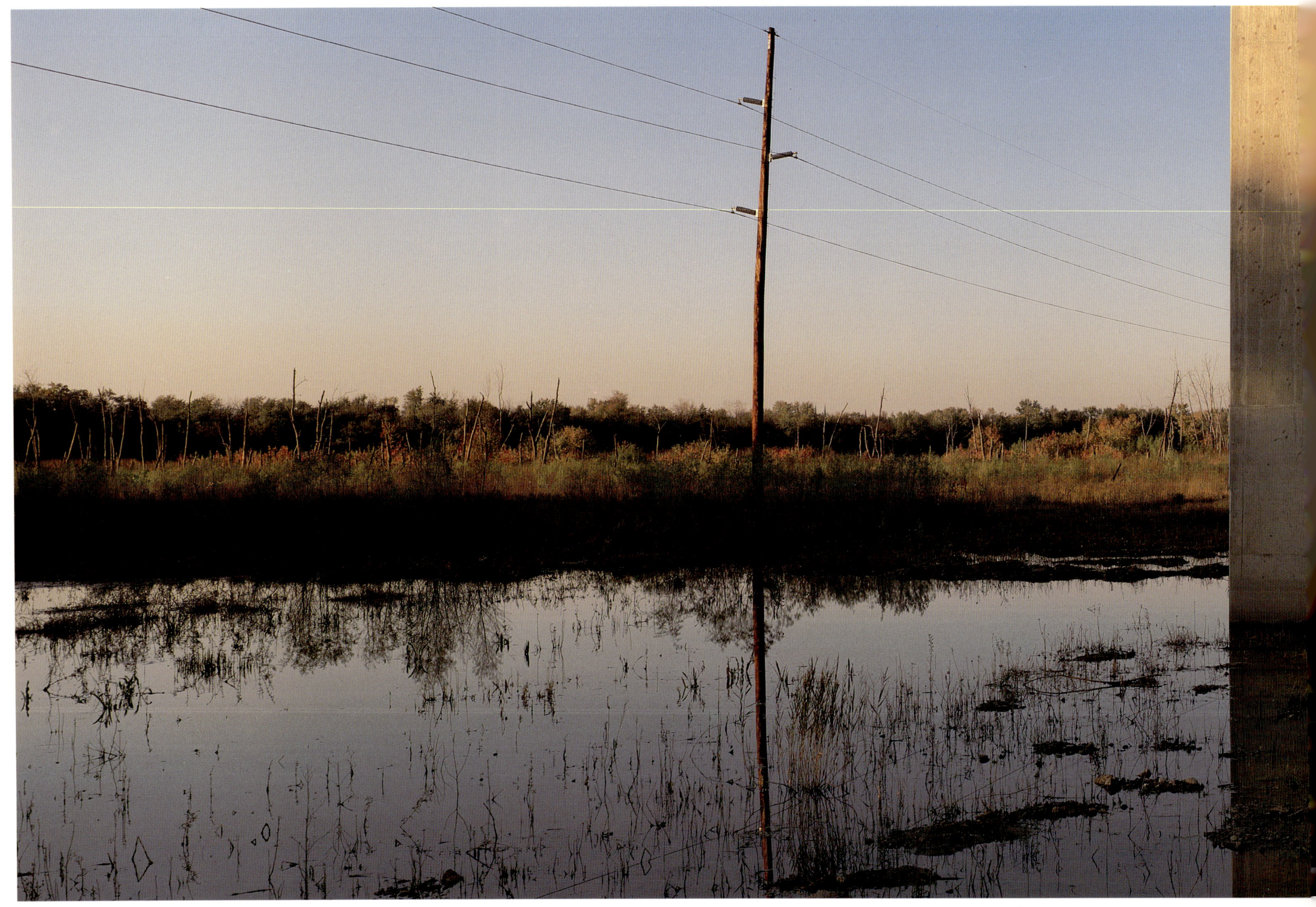

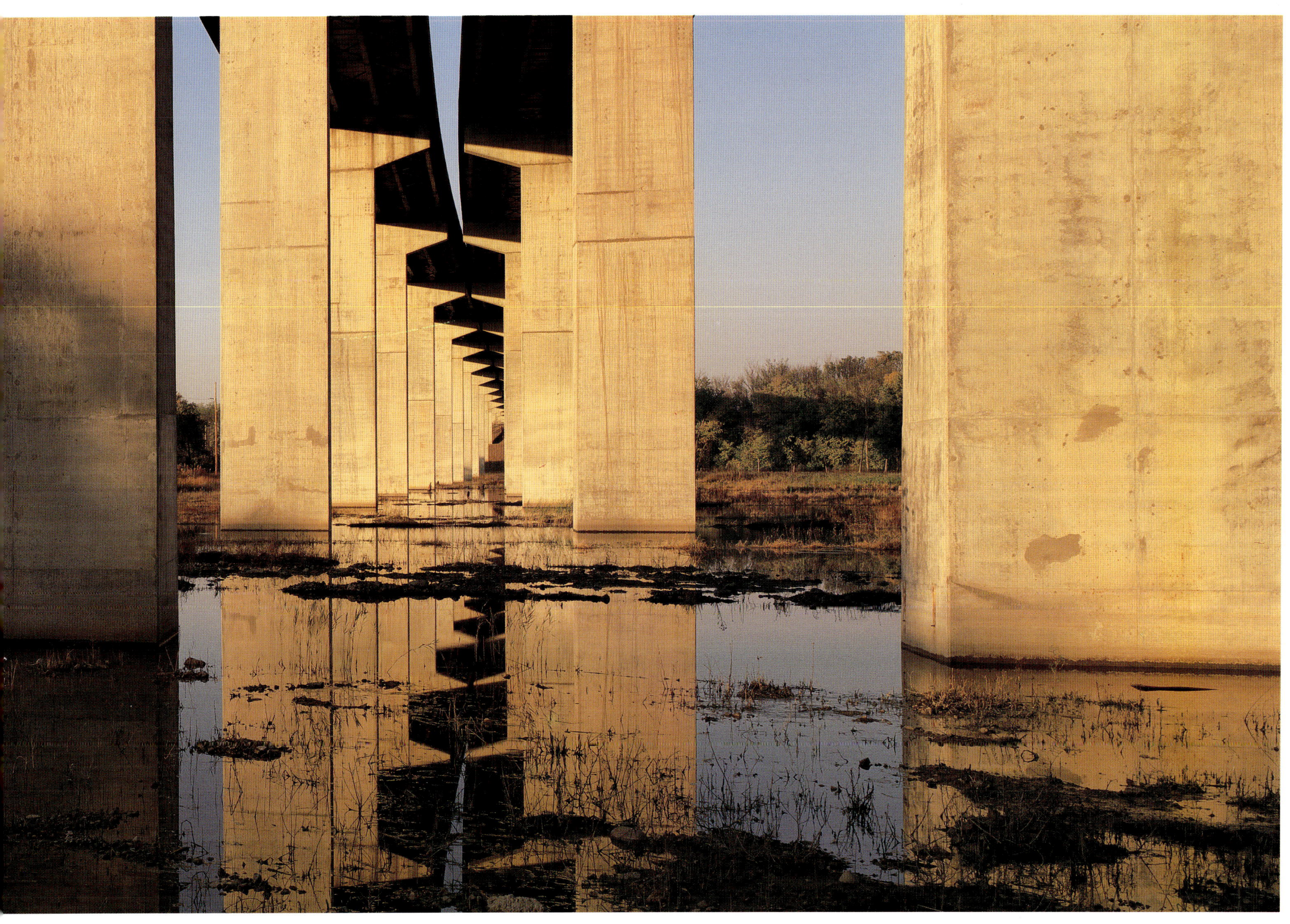

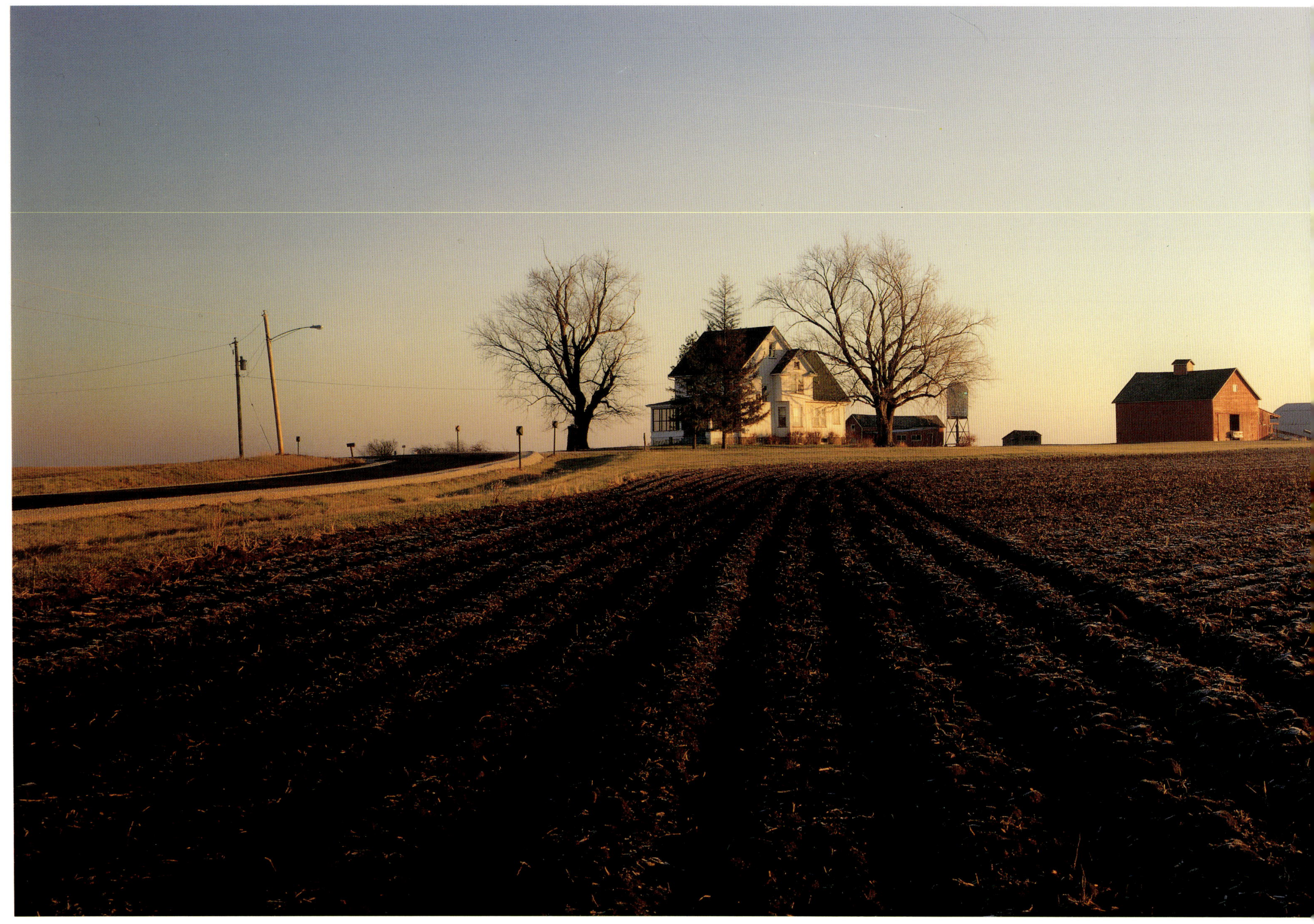

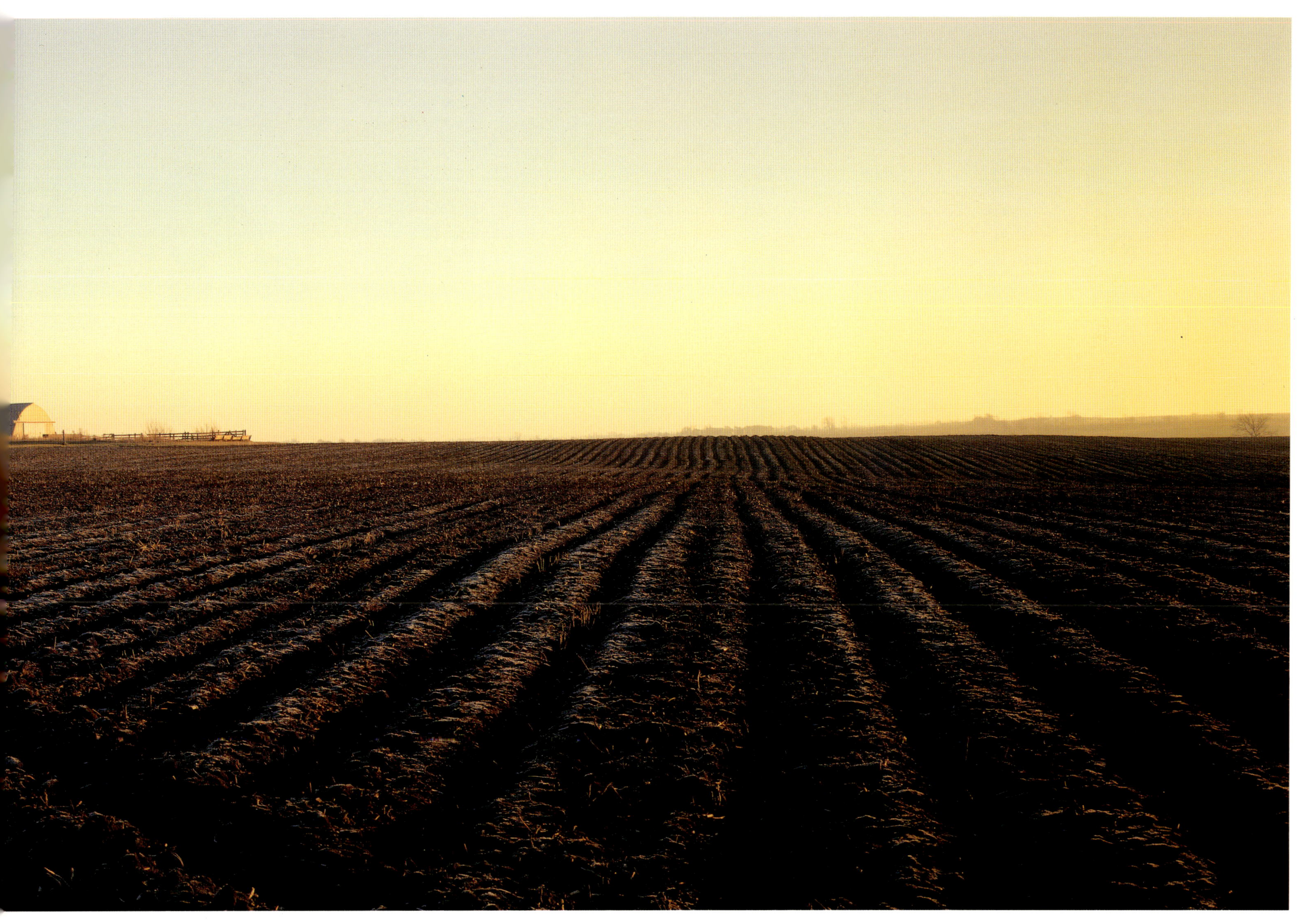

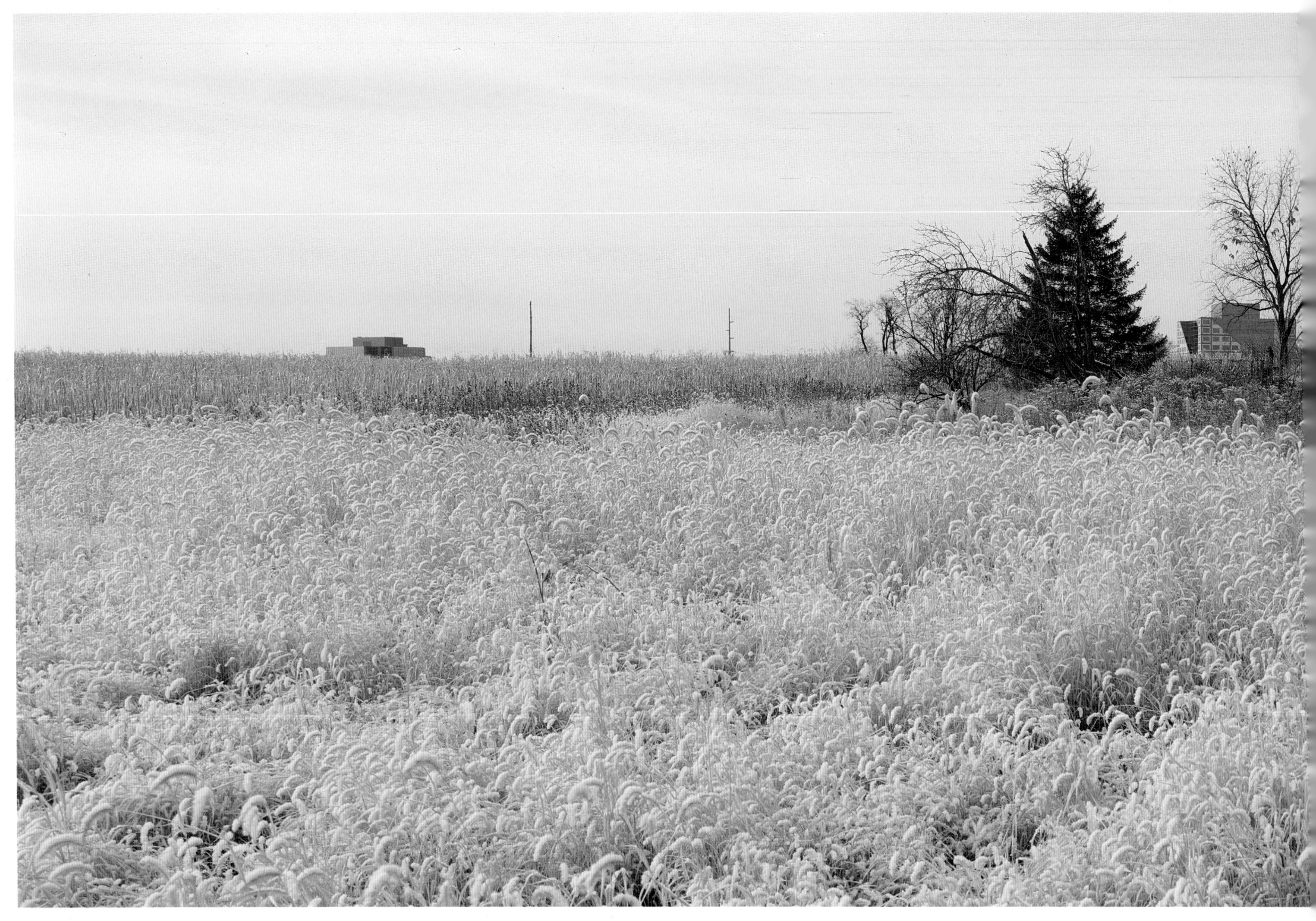

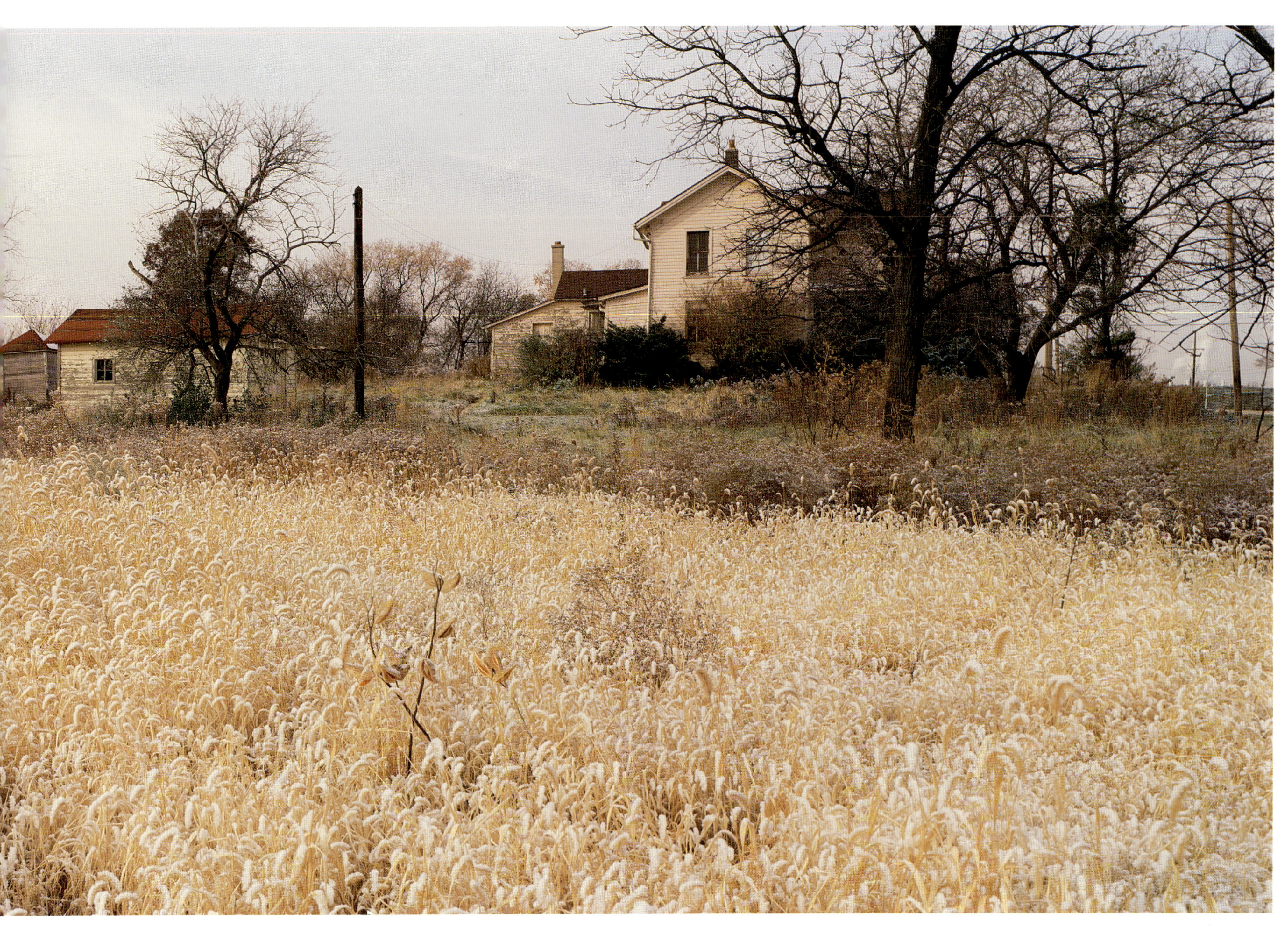

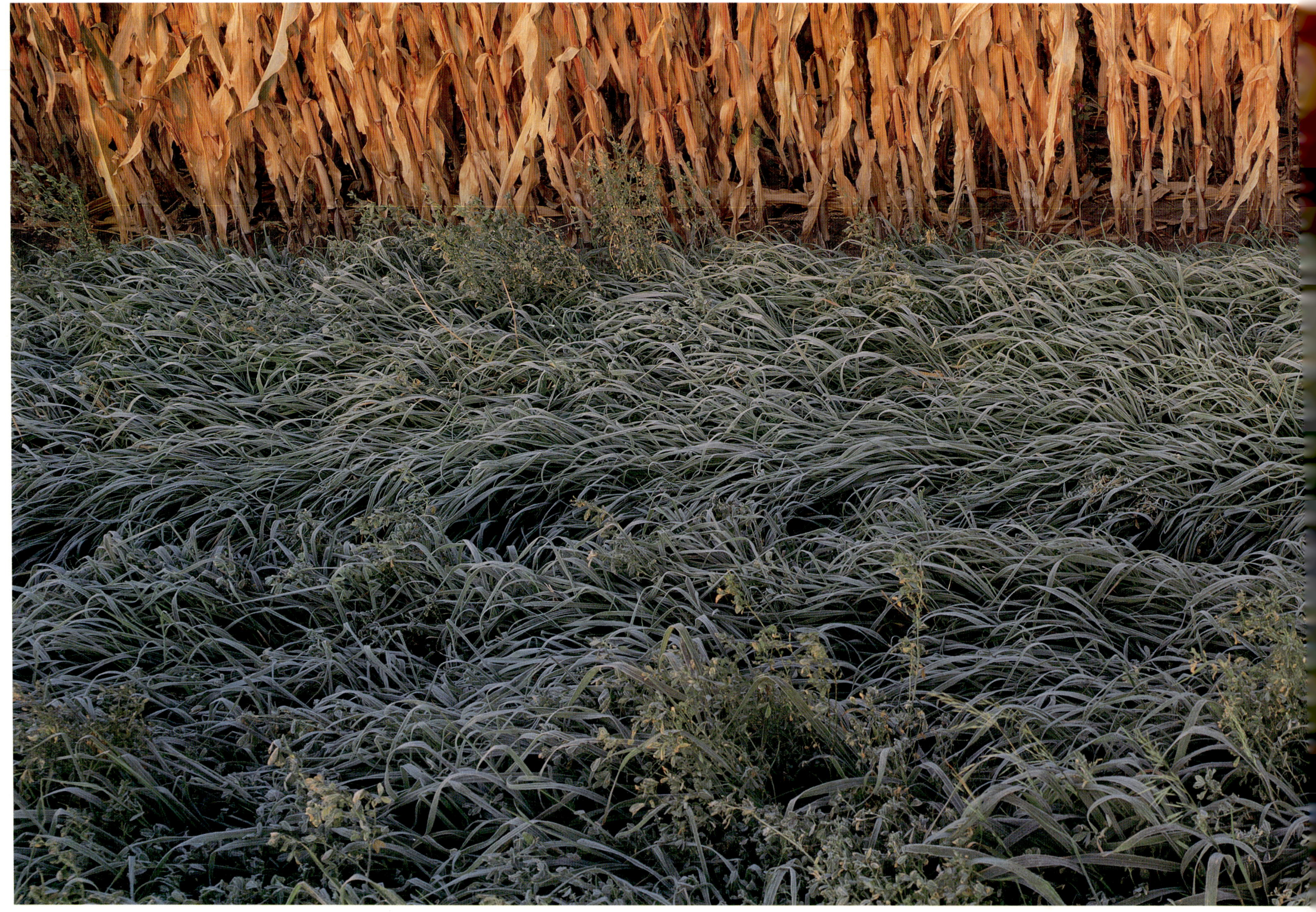

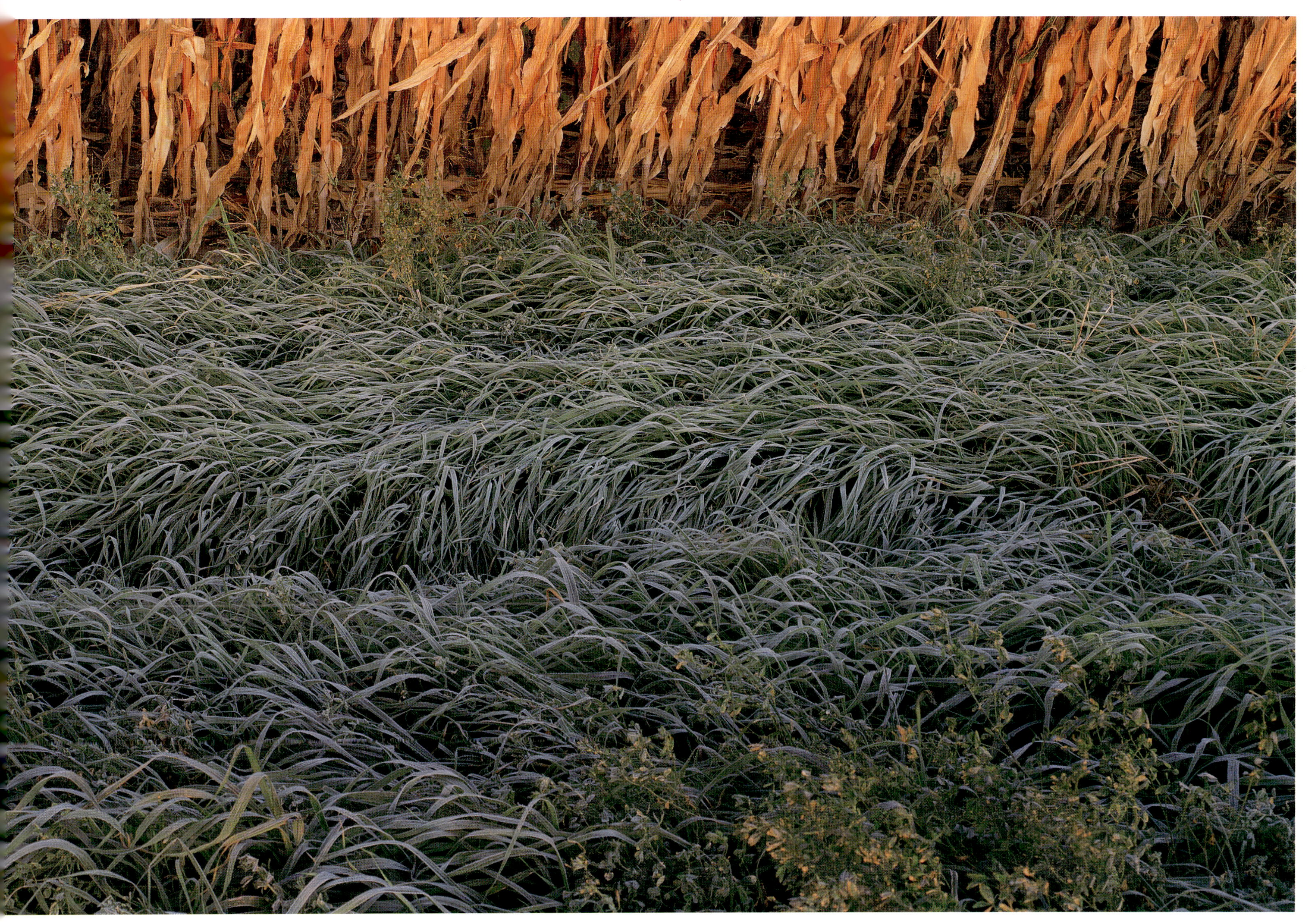

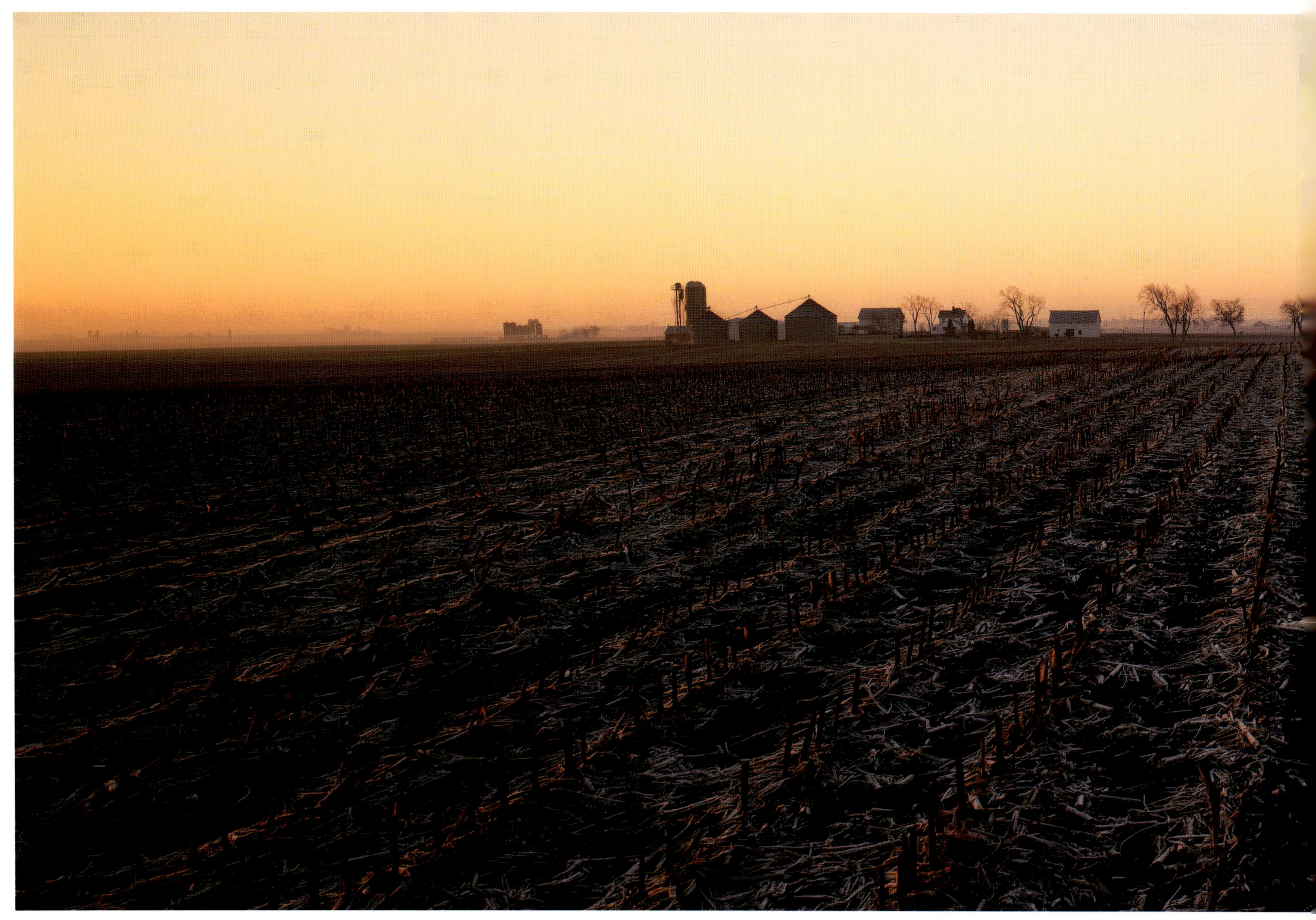

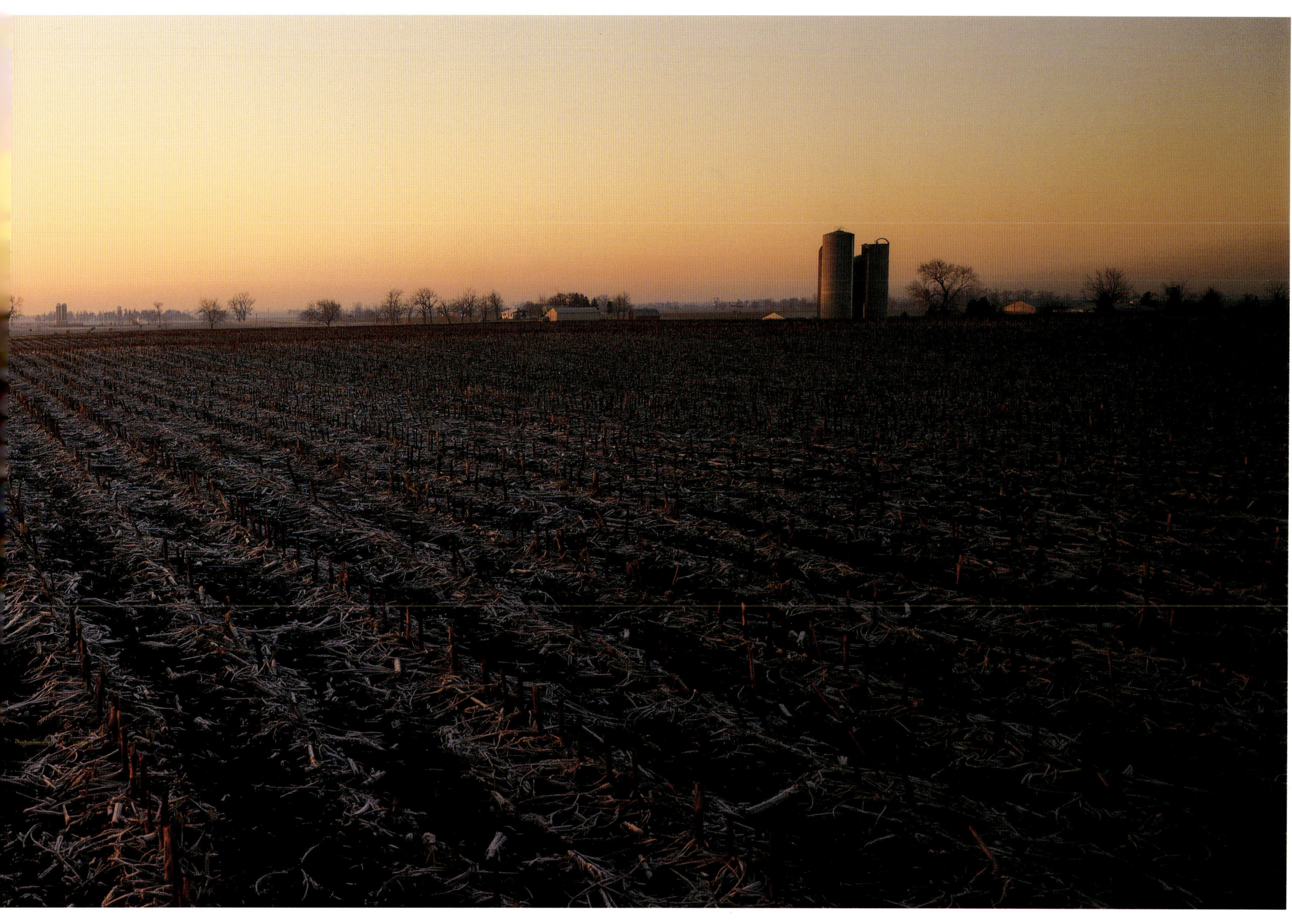

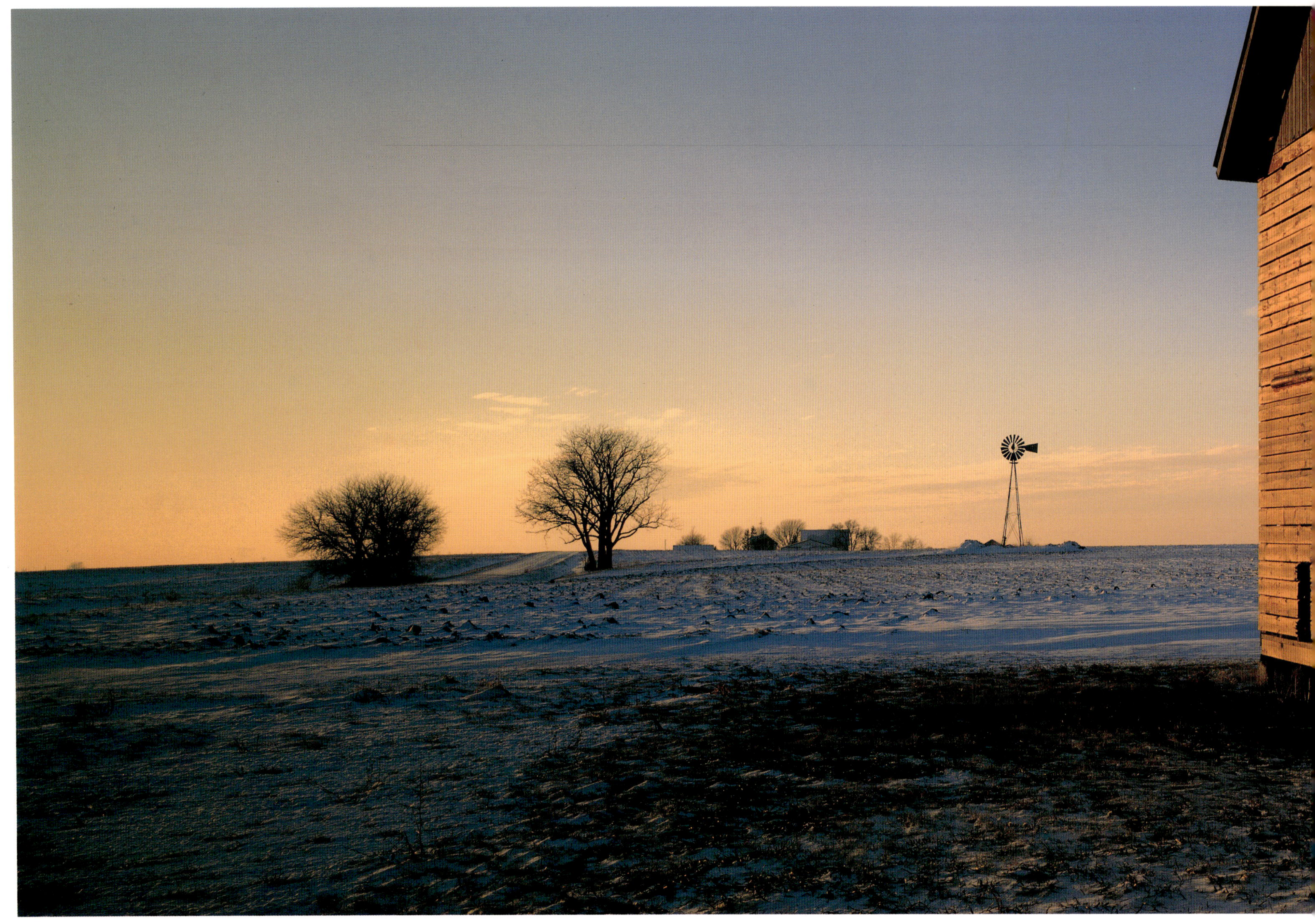

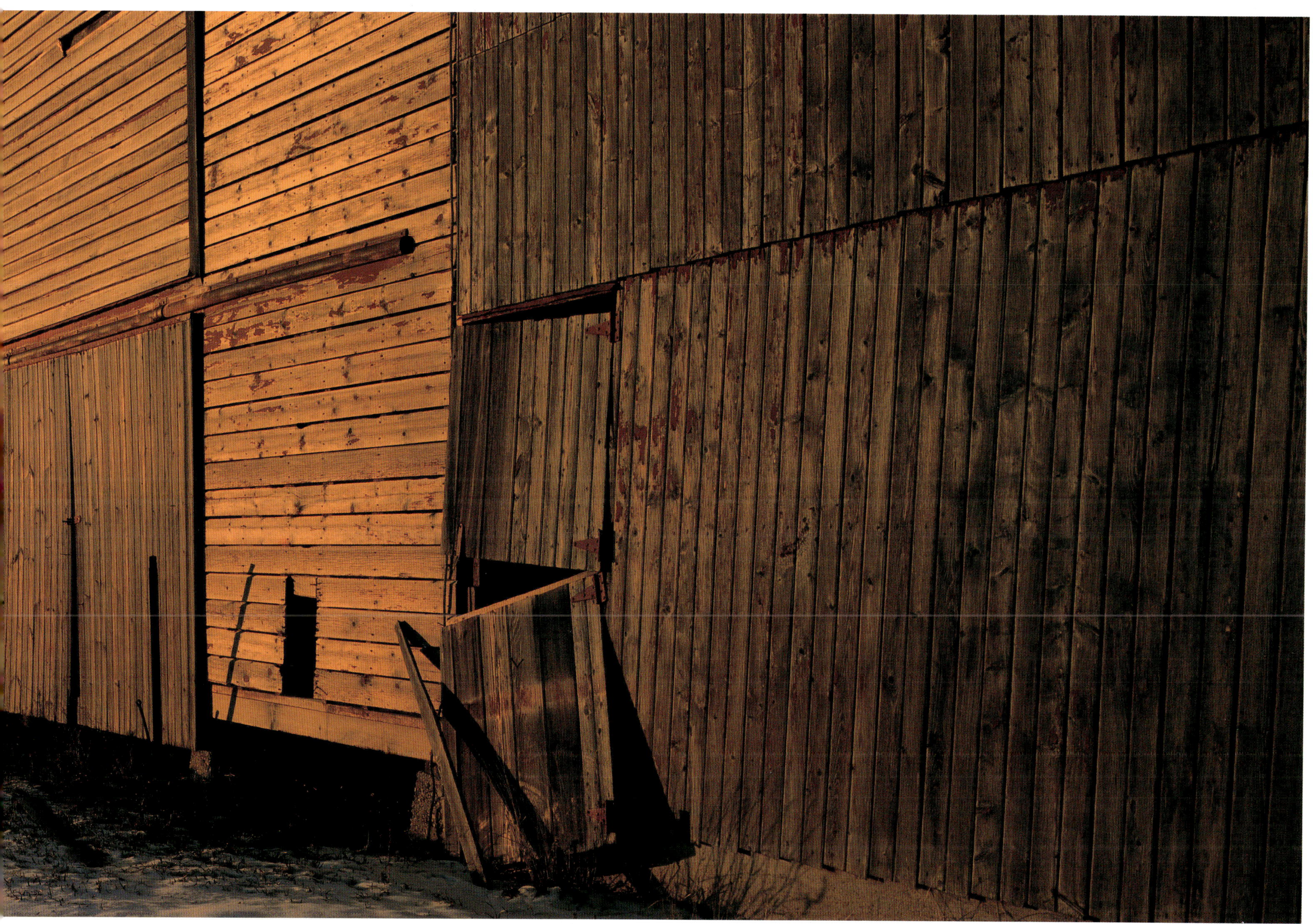

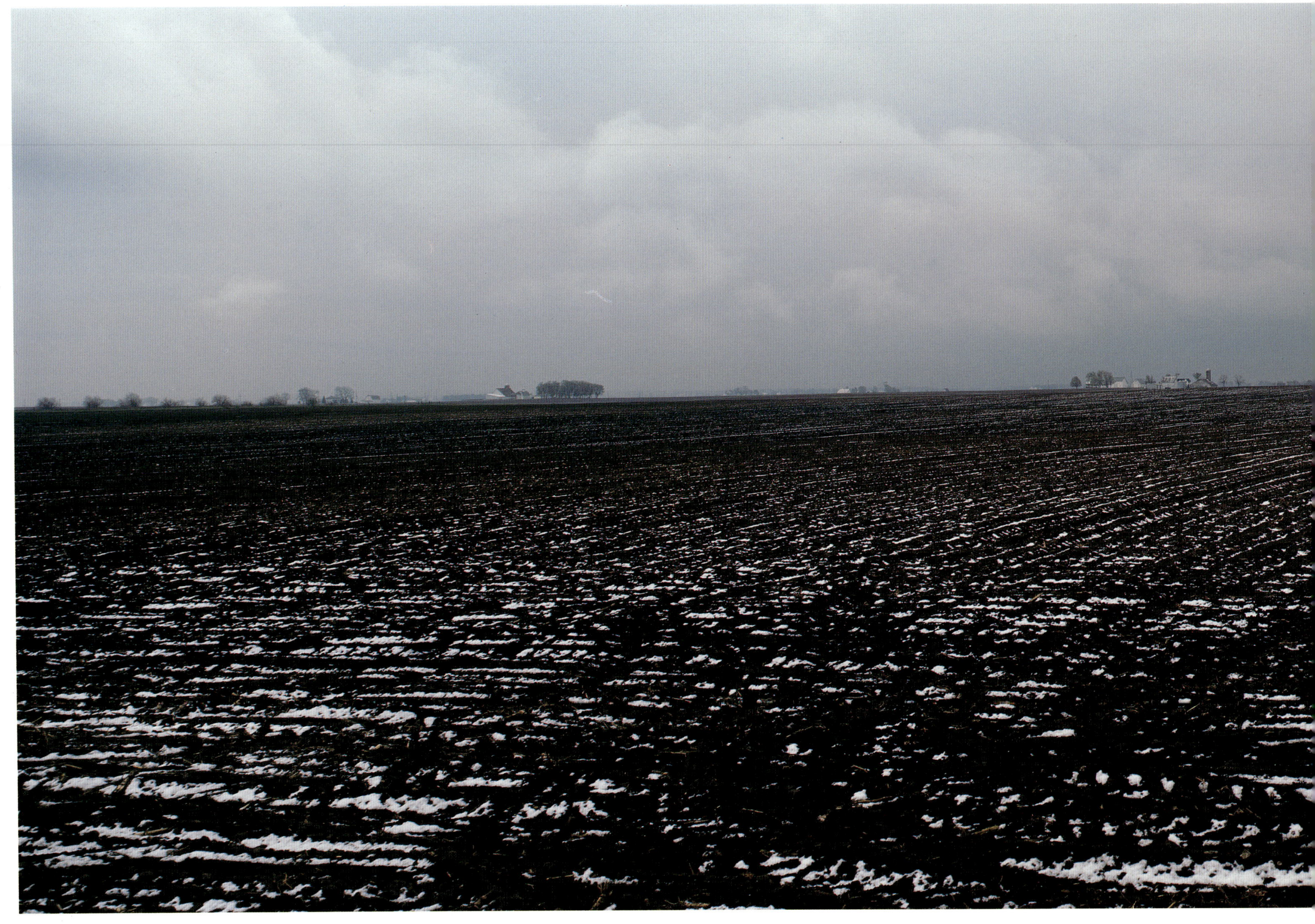

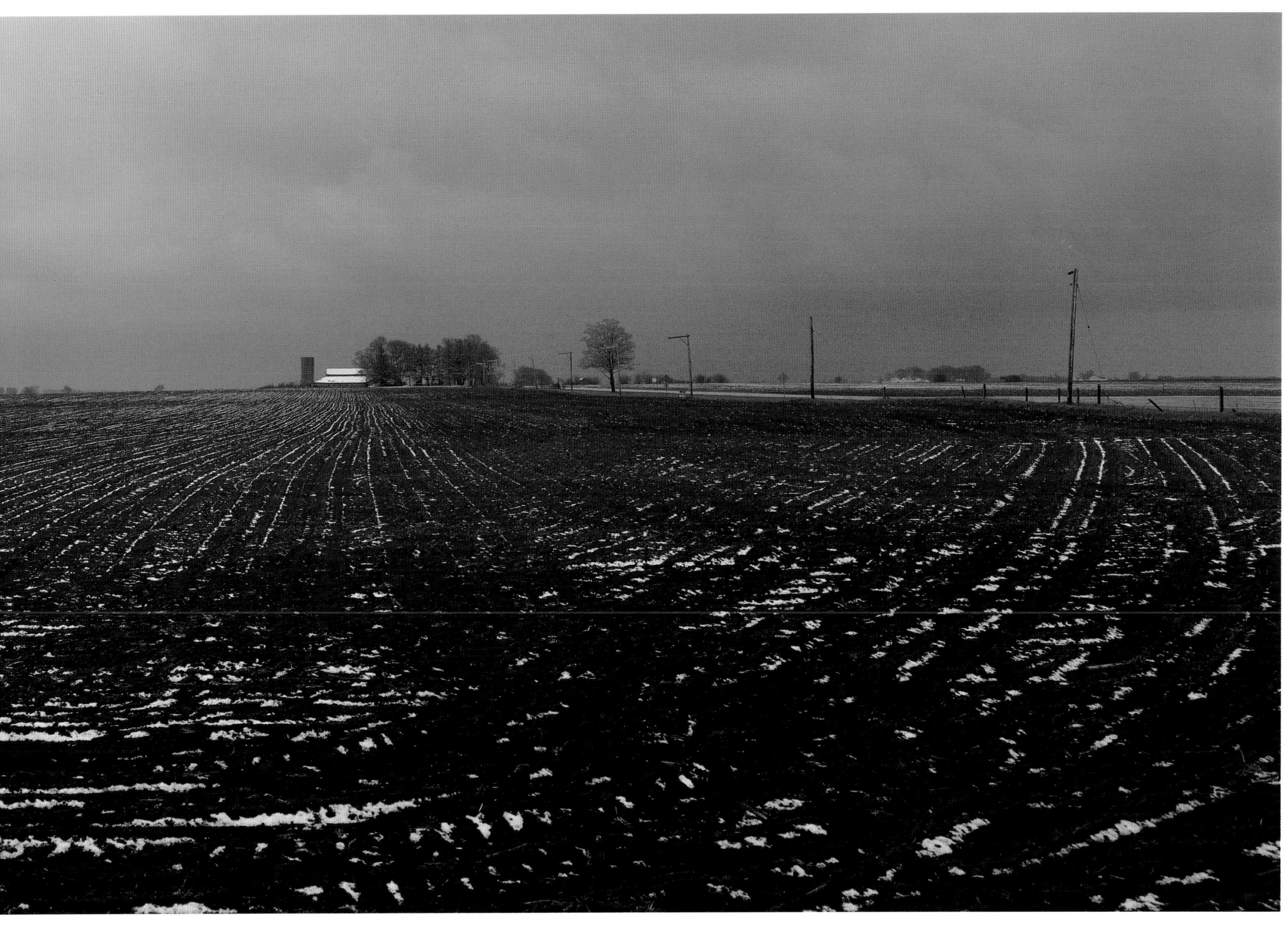

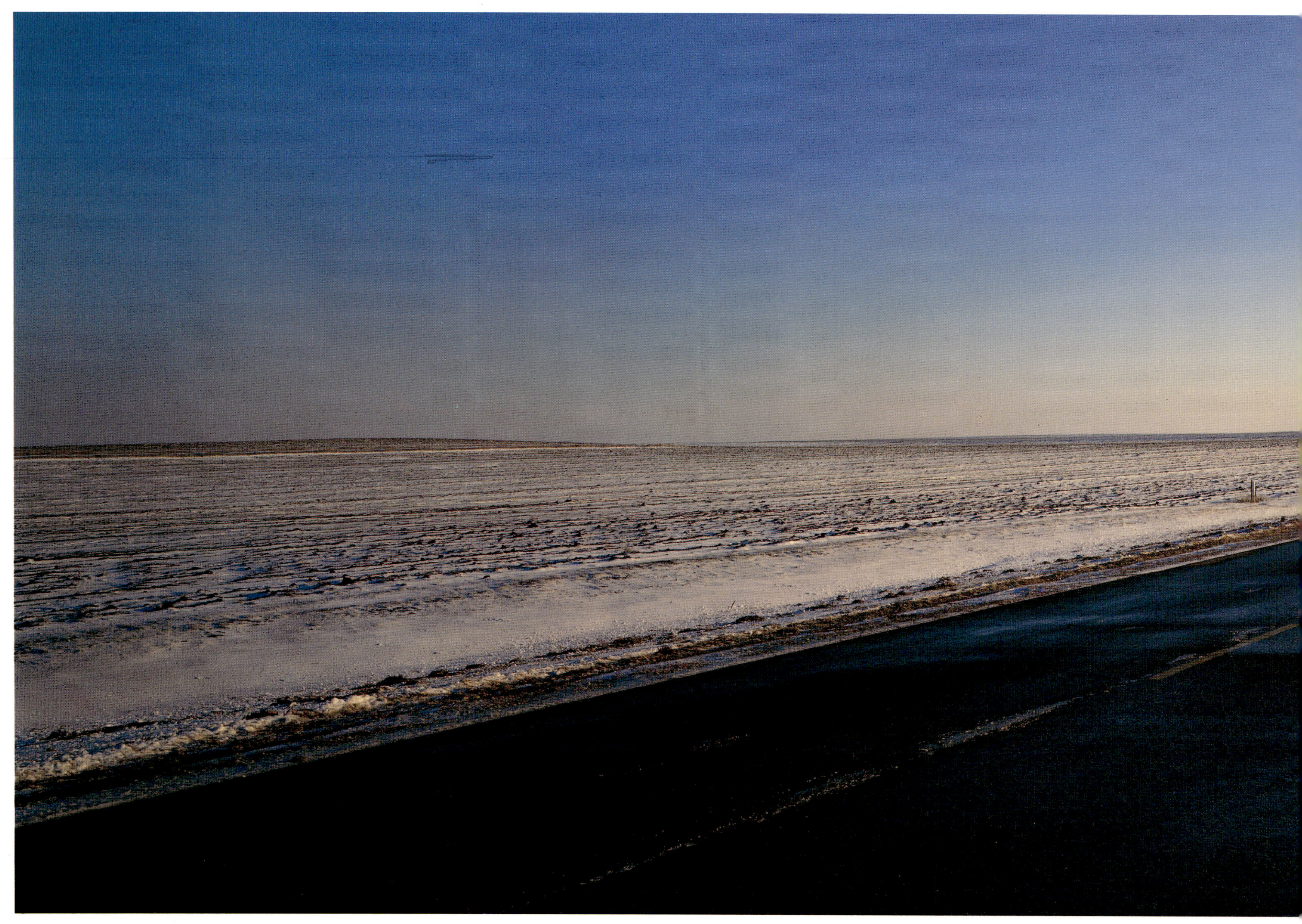

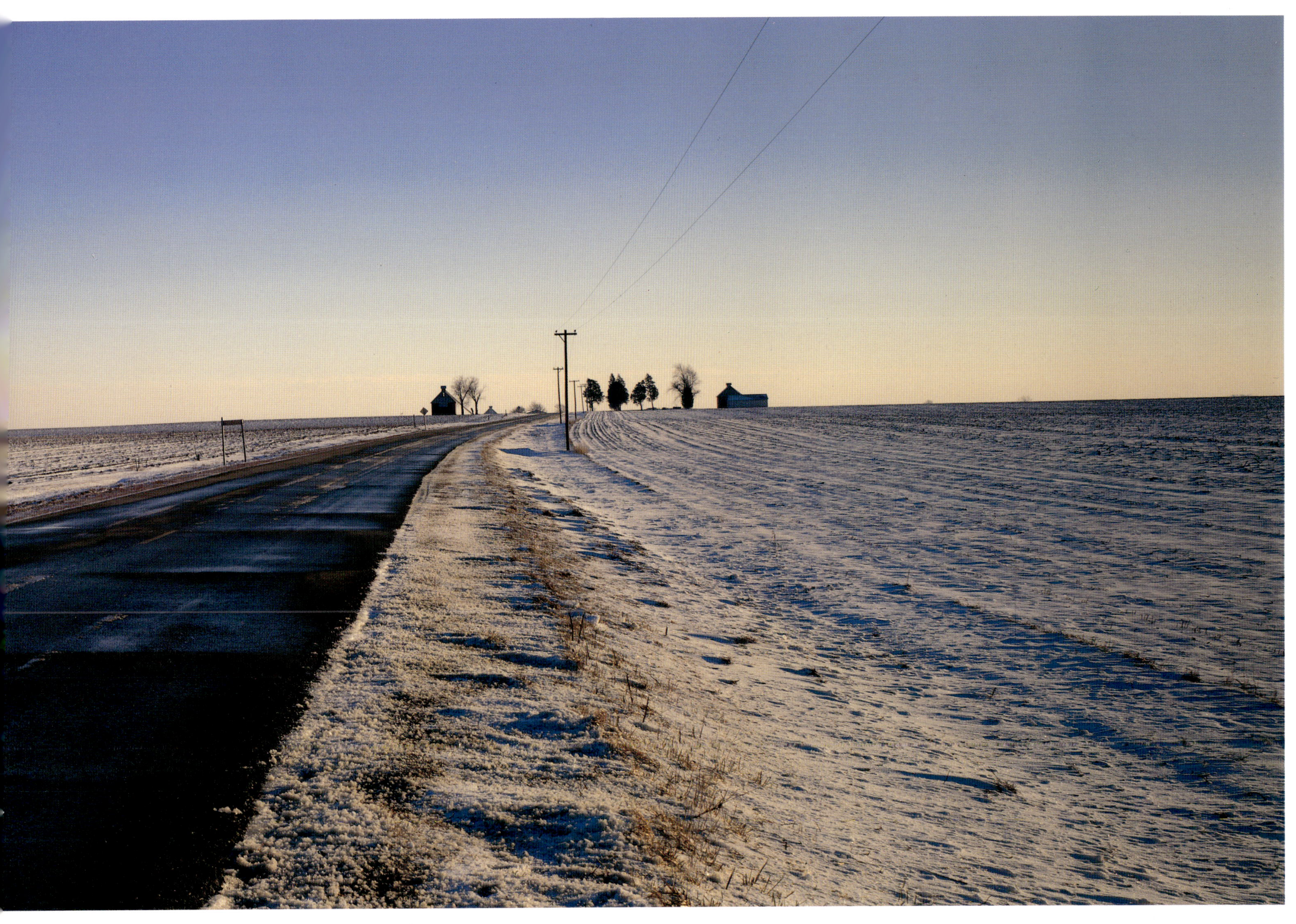

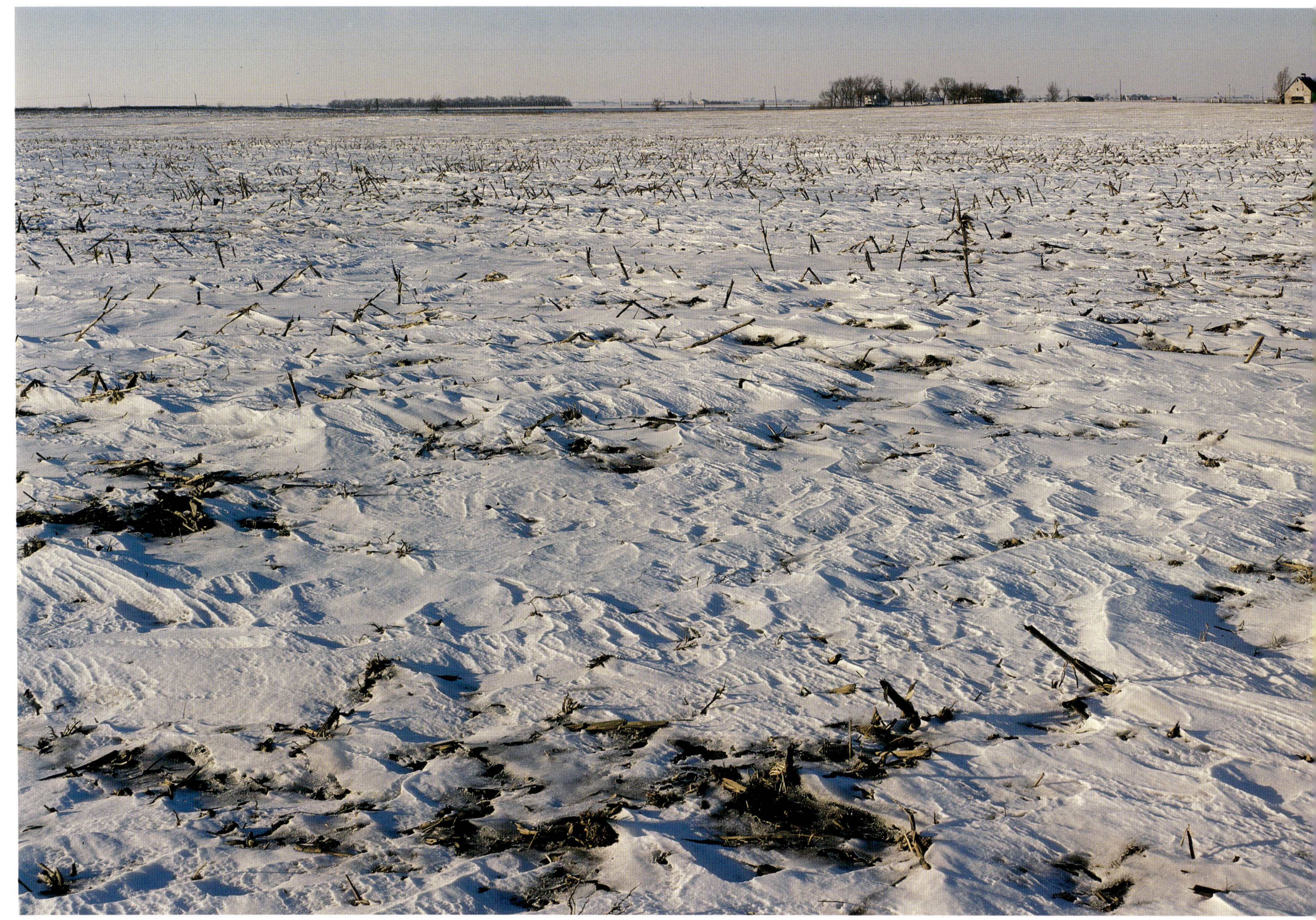

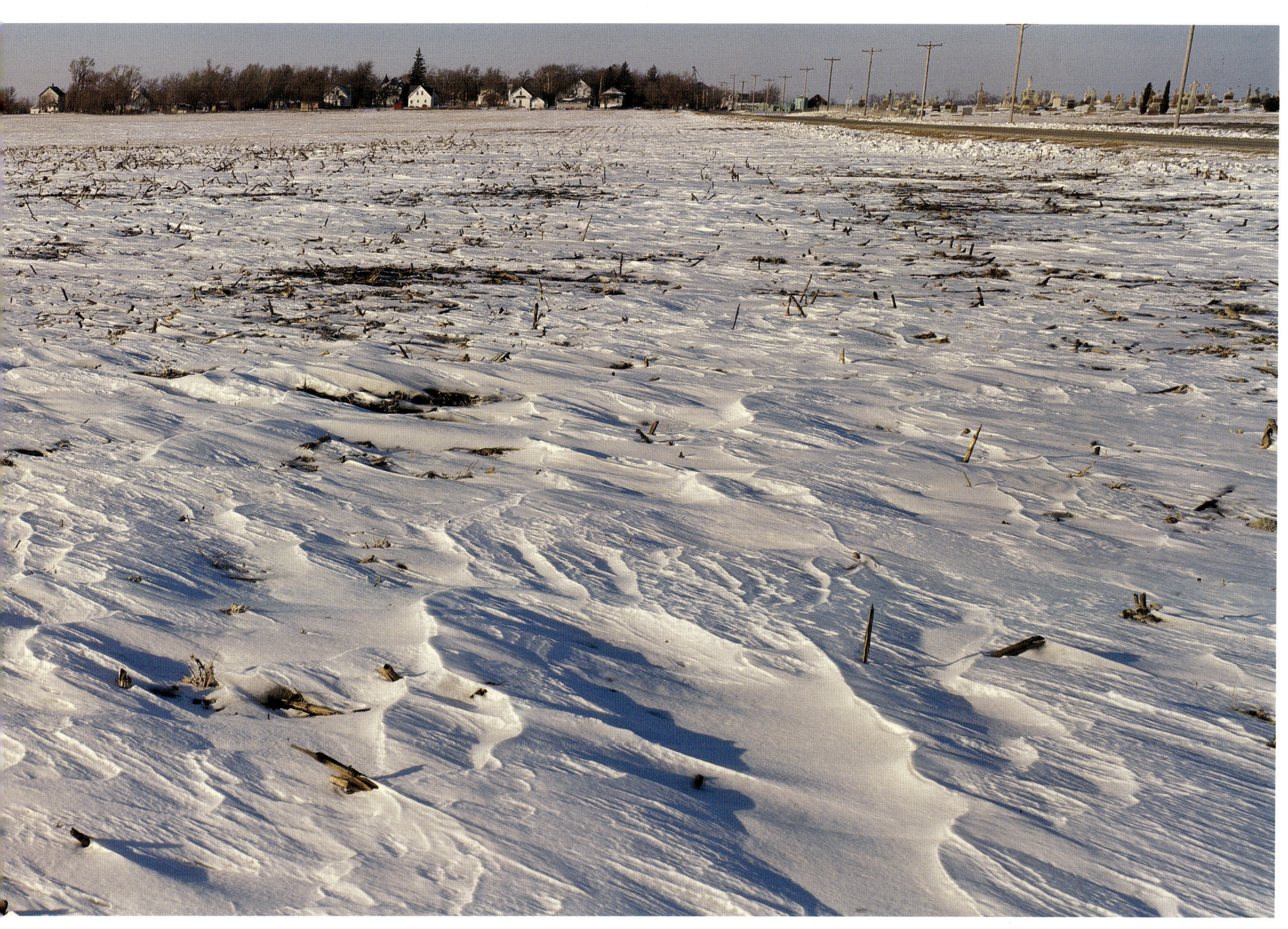

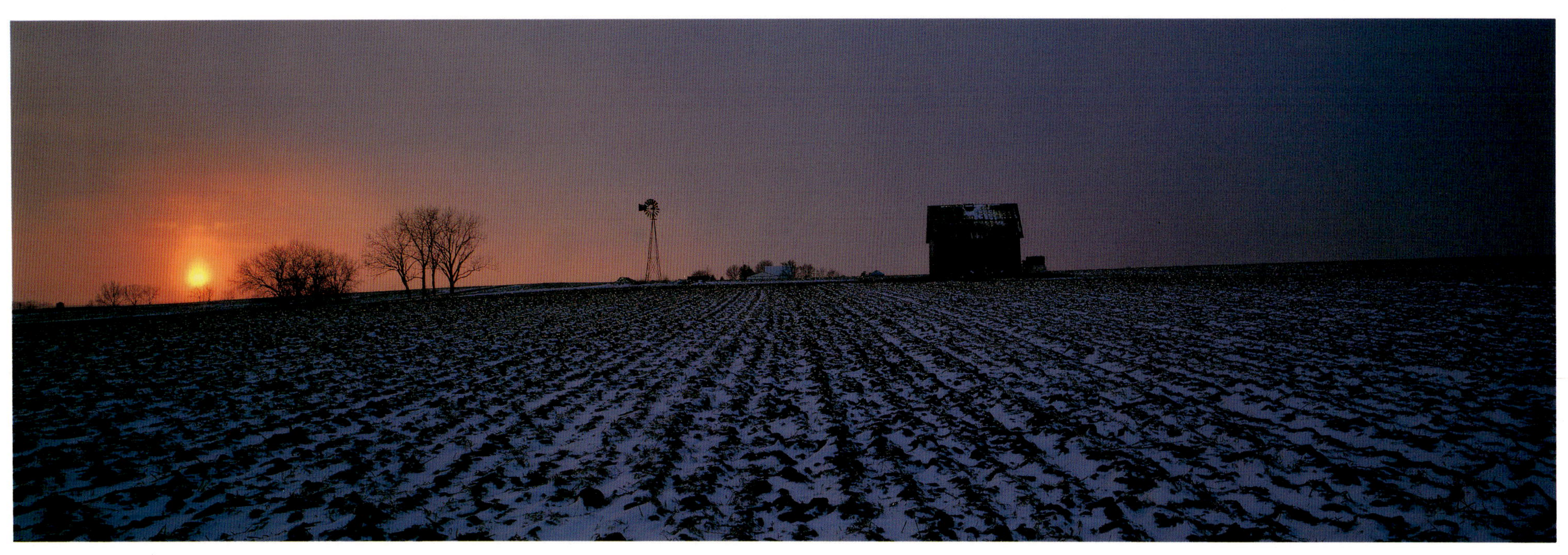

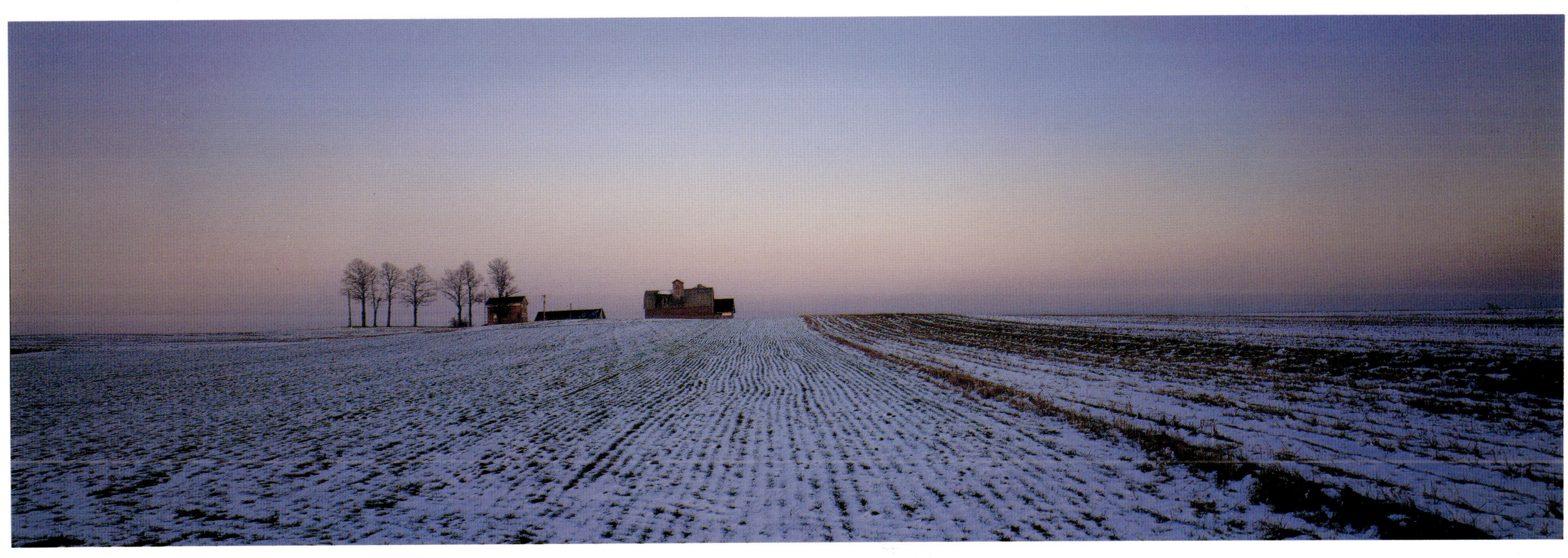

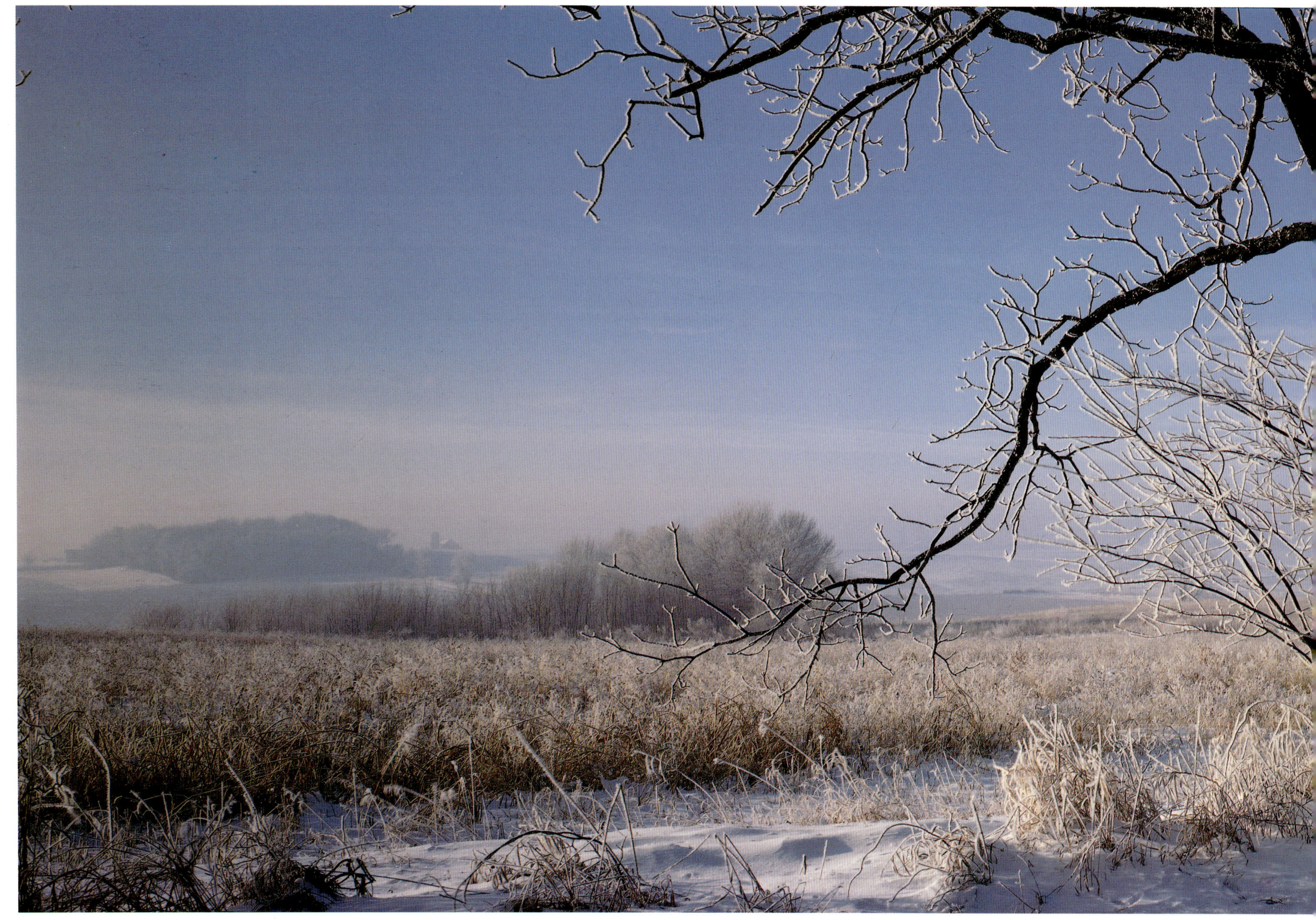

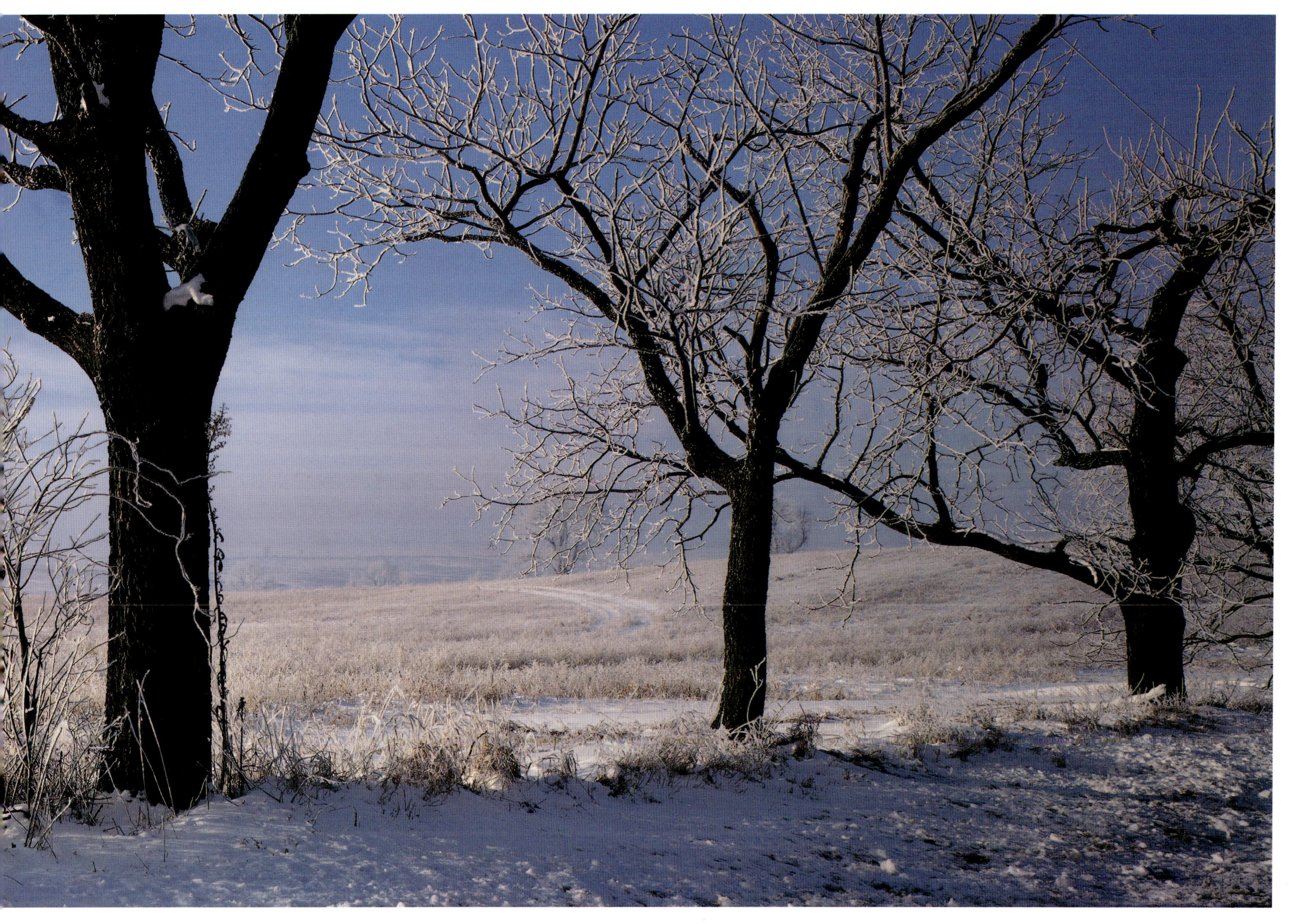

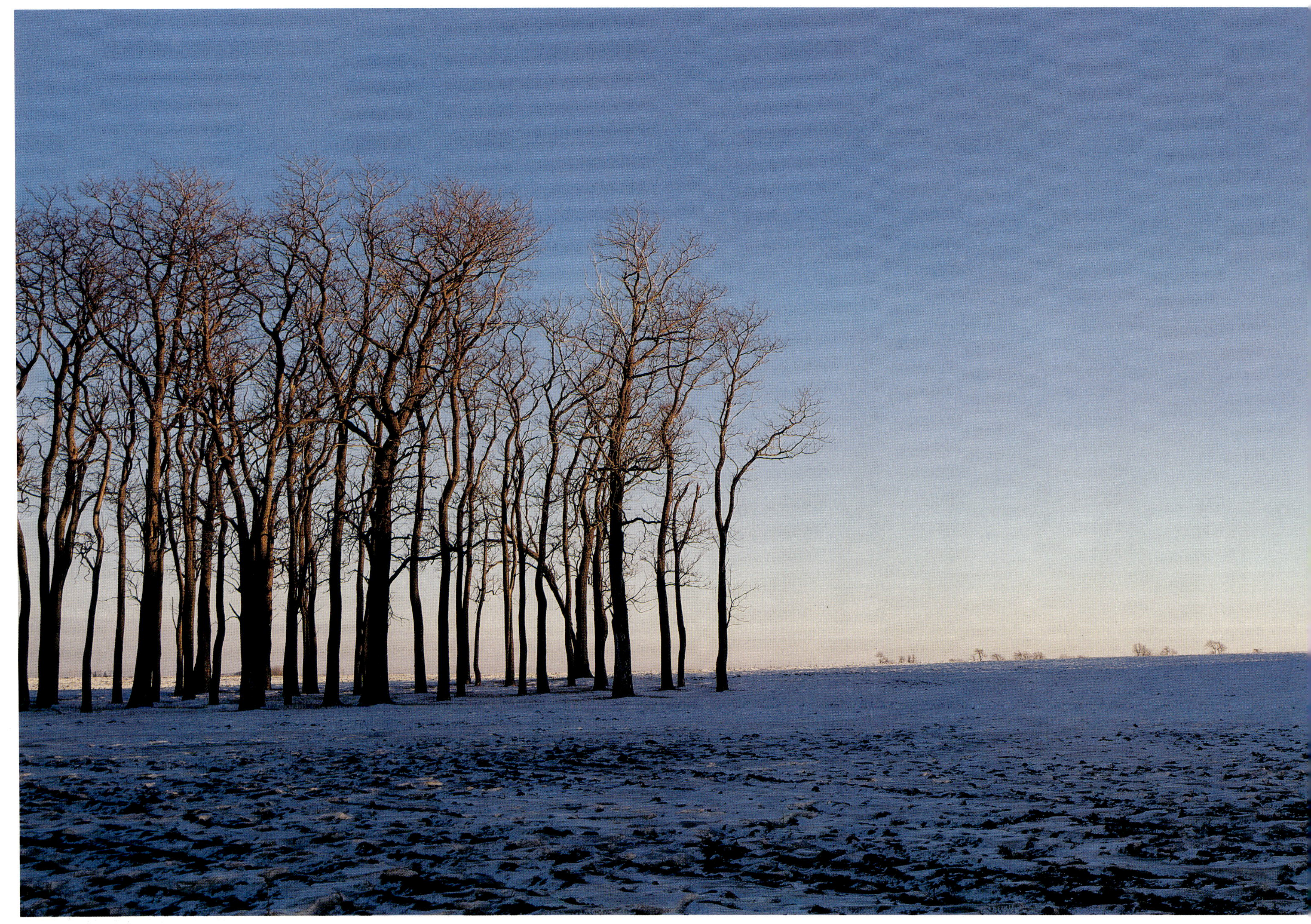

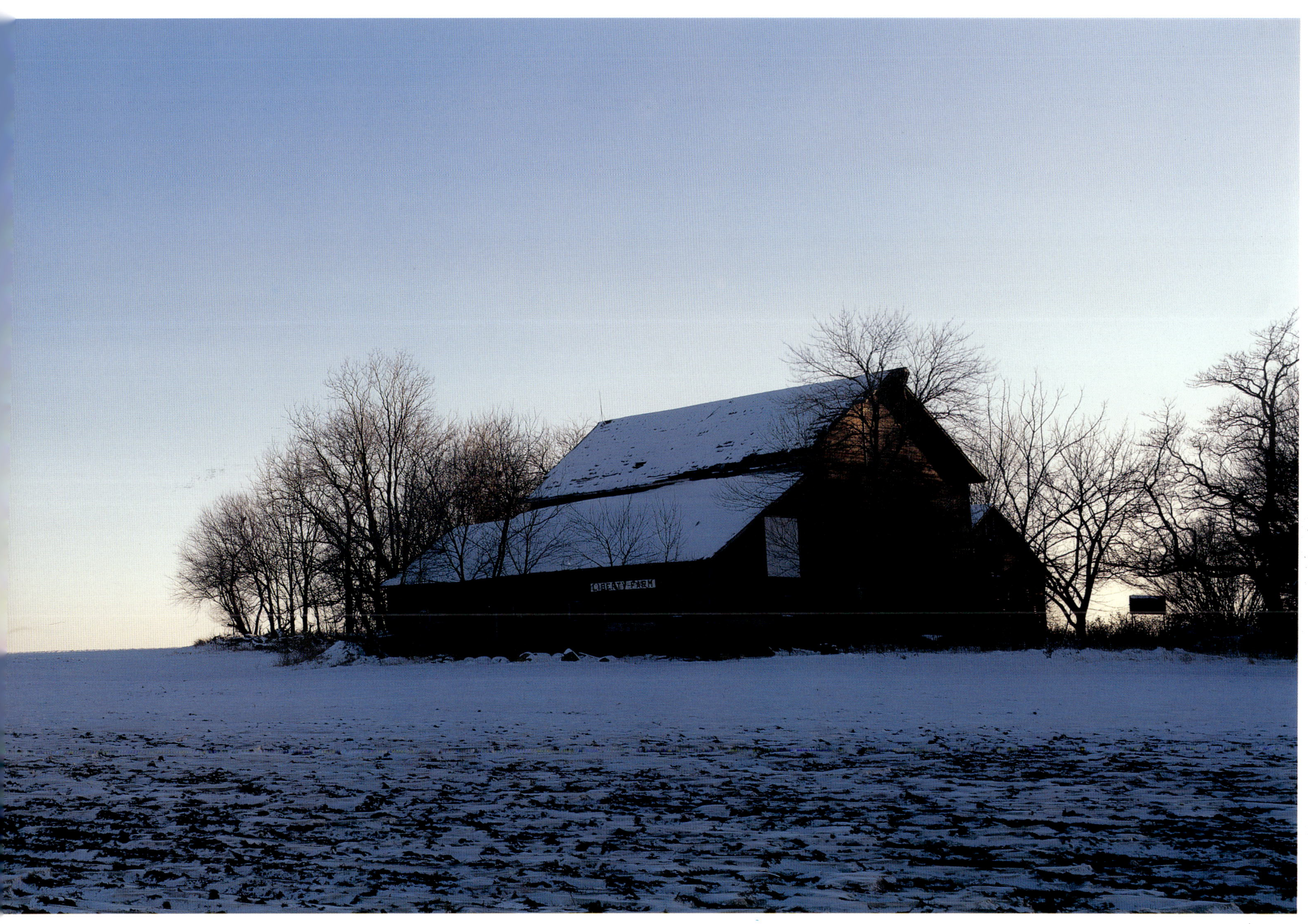
LIBERTY FARM

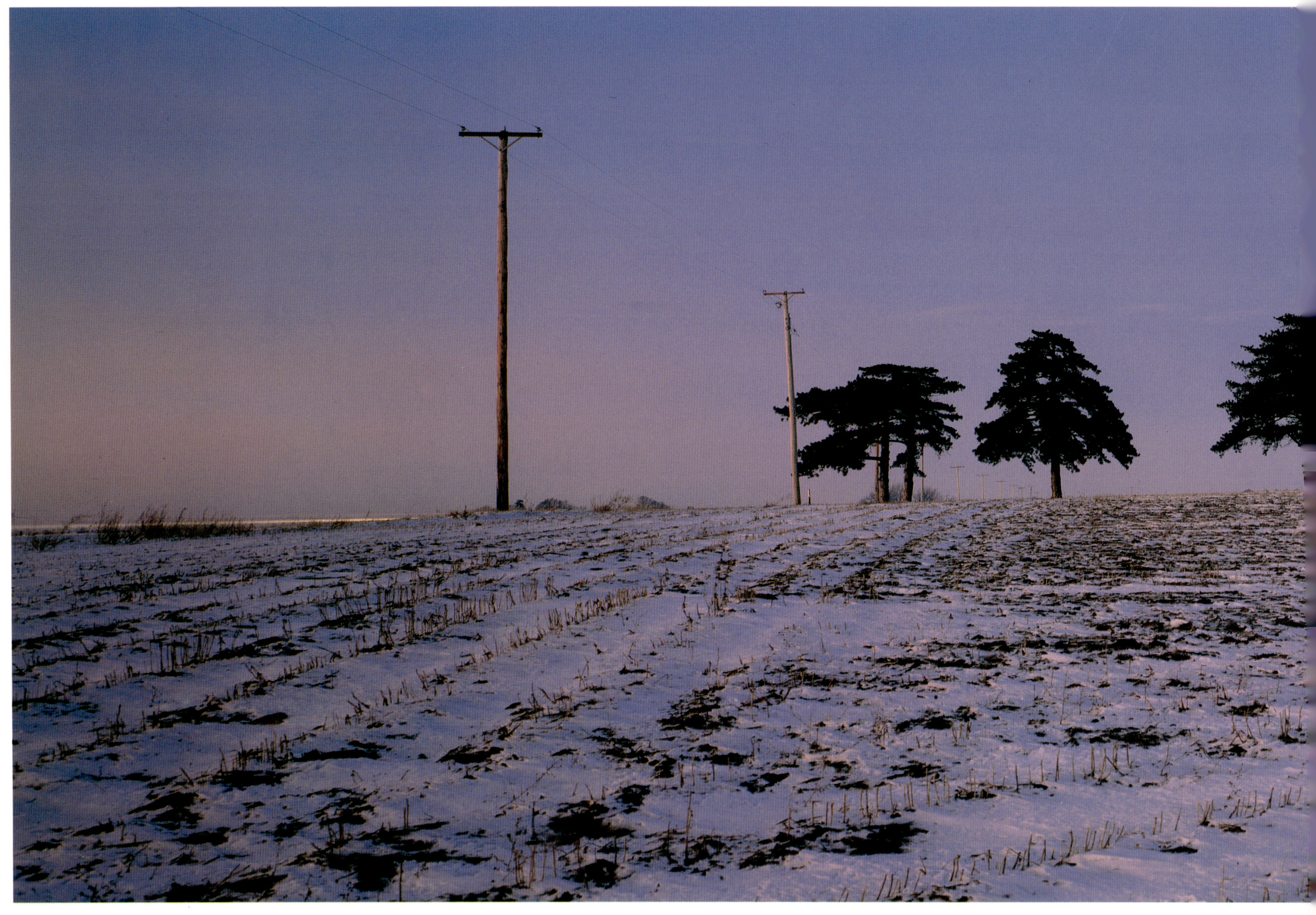

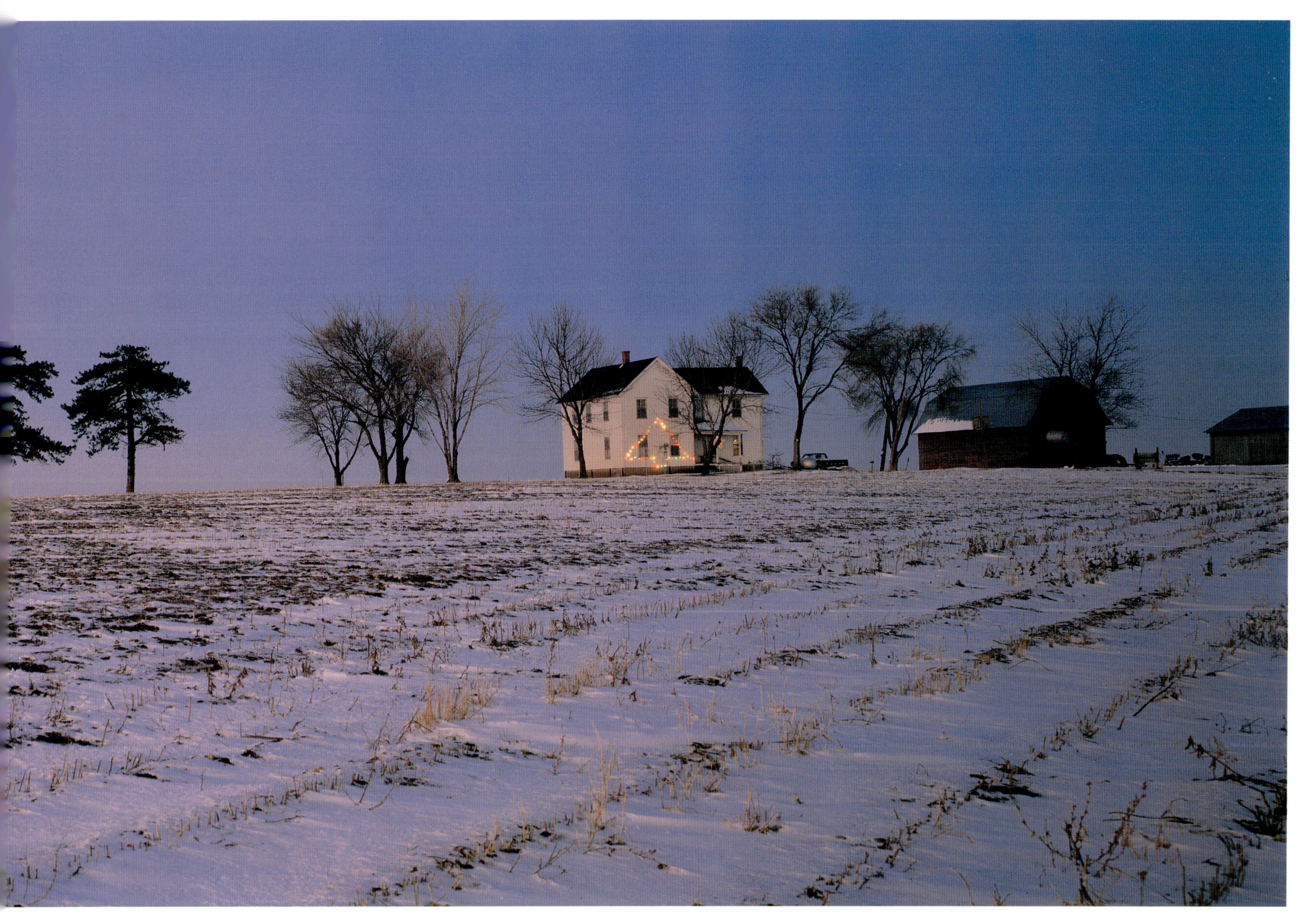

The Photographs

1 Near Woodbine, Jo Daviess County
2 South of Yorkville, Kendall County
3 Redbud, early spring, Johnson County
4 Castle Rock, along the Rock River, Ogle County
5 Early morning field, Cumberland County
6 Moonrise, DuPage County
7 Rock River, early spring, Ogle County
8 Early morning, looking toward Chatsworth, Livingston County
9 Storm clouds, Jo Daviess County
10 Lake Ellyn in fog, DuPage County
11 Field and barn, Livingston County
12 Tree along Rural Route 1, Champaign County
13 Ravine off Highway 71, LaSalle County
14 Oaks in foggy pasture, Moultrie County
15 Late afternoon near Tuscola, Douglas County
16 Old fence with young goldenrod, early summer, Kane County
17 Mustard field and blue sky, DeWitt County
18 Grove east of Oregon, Ogle County, ten minutes before dawn
19 Grove east of Oregon, Ogle County, ten minutes after dawn
20 Early morning fog and old farm along Glidden Road, DeKalb County
21 Sun burning through fog, west of Sycamore, DeKalb County
22 Cottonwoods and farm at sunset, north of Newark, Kendall County
23 Sunflower field north of Melvin, Livingston County
24 Early morning, east of Mt. Morris, Ogle County
25 Country ballfield south of Arthur, Moultrie County
26 Old filling station, Arcola, Douglas County
27 Rock River, Ogle County
28 Post office at dusk, Table Grove, Fulton County
29 Fallen oak tree, Stephenson County
30 U.S. 64, west of Sycamore, Ogle County

31 Cadwell grain elevator, Moultrie County
32 Misty forest along the Rock River, near Grand Detour, Ogle County
33 Grain elevator, Woodford County
34 Twilight reflected in windows, Ford County
35 Warehouse building with blue door, Chatsworth, Livingston County
36 Open field and clouds, Hayworth, McLean County
37 Picket fence and farm, McLean County
38 Cornfield, Lee County
39 Pumpkin field on Condill Farm, Moultrie County
40 Storefronts, Chatsworth, Livingston County
41 Moon in twilight, Elburn, Kane County
42 Predawn glow, south of Plainfield, Kendall County
43 Abandoned train station, Woodford County
44 Hilltop cemetery, Livingston County
45 Autumn in Herrick Lake Forest Preserve, DuPage County
46 Farm at dusk, DeKalb County
47 Concrete bridge supports and wetland, LaSalle County
48 Frost on plowed fields, Grundy County
49 Dusting of snow, farm on Warrenville Road, near Naperville
50 Early morning frost, Moultrie County
51 Frost on open field, Kendall County
52 Windmill and old barn, Livingston County
53 Snow on field near Genoa, DeKalb County
54 Large field along county road, Livingston County
55 Snowfield near Campus, Livingston County
56 Winter sunset, Livingston County
57 Farm in winter, Kane County
58 Hoarfrost on trees and field south of Burlington, Kane County
59 Field of snow and catalpa grove near Batavia, Kane County
60 Farmhouse with Christmas lights, north of Campus, Livingston County

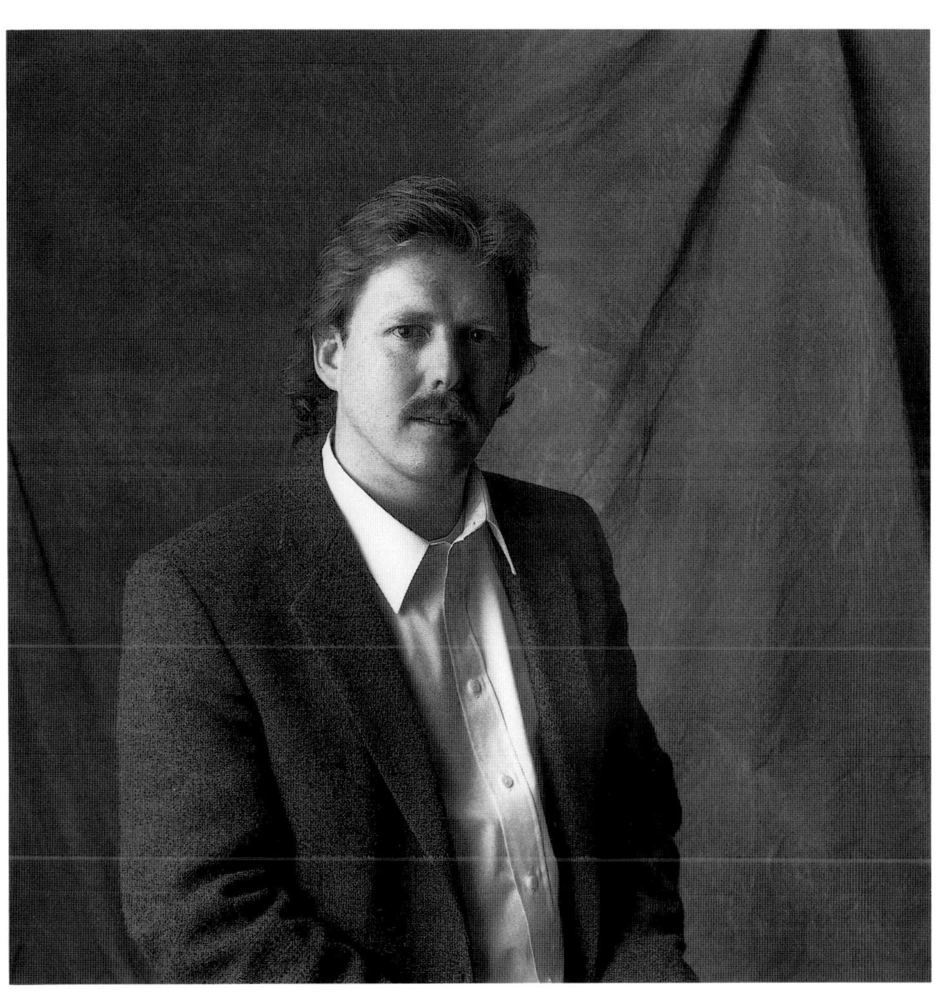

About the Photographer

Gary Irving is an award-winning travel photographer based near Chicago. He has become renowned for his eloquent interpretation of the Midwestern landscape. Mr. Irving has photographed throughout the country and has three previous books to his credit, including *Illinois,* but in *Beneath an Open Sky* he explores fully for the first time his newfound fascination with the panoramic format.

All the photographs in this book were taken using a Fuji G617 Panorama camera with a 105 mm f8 Fujinon wide-angle lens yielding a 60 mm x 170 mm image.

The film chosen was Fujichrome 50 Professional 120; no filtration was used.

Acknowledgments

I would like to express my appreciation to Richard Wentworth, Director of the University of Illinois Press, for believing in this project; to Larry Slanker, Art Director at the Press, for his sensitivity to the presentation of the photographs; and to the rest of the staff for their involvement. Thanks go to Ray Bial for his cooperation in writing an introduction and for his generous input in some of the decision making and image selection. I am grateful to the numerous people I met along the road who allowed me to photograph their farms and who offered warm conversation. I would especially like to thank the numerous friends and relatives who encouraged me to spend the time necessary to document the beauty found in the Midwest.